Business Principles and Practices

(From Rags to Riches)

"Broke Yesterday…Rich Today…

By Alisha Broughton, M.ED.

Business Principles and Practices

(From Rags to Riches) "Broke Yesterday...Rich Today...

By: Alisha Broughton, M.ED.

Cover Designed By: Jazzy Kitty Publishing

Cover images: www.photobucket.com

Logo Designs By: Andre M. Saunders

Editor: Alisha Broughton

Co-Editor: Anelda Attaway

© 2012 Alisha Broughton

ISBN 978-0-9851453-8-5

Library of Congress Control Number: 2012956202

For Worldwide Distribution. Printed in the United States of America. Published by Jazzy Kitty Greetings Marketing & Publishing, LLC. Utilizing Microsoft Publishing Software. Please be advise this book has strong lanuage and content.

ACKNOWLEDGEMENTS

"First, acknowledging My Lord and Savior, Jesus Christ without him none of this would be made possible."

I would to say, "Thank you, to my mom Beverly Singletary and my Step-Father Benjamin Singletary for all of their love and support over the years, without my family none of this would be possible. "Thanks to my daughter's Ashley and Amber Broughton for editing, and re-editing. My dad Vaun-Dyke Ford and my brothers Bryan Broughton, Benjamin Singletary Jr., Damien Showell, Shawn Godwin and Troy Cropper. All of my nieces and nephews, to many to mentioned. Auntie, loves you all! I appreciate all of your wonderful suggestions. Thank you to Apostle Ivory Hopkins, and Minister Evelyn Hopkins, you never doubt me and you always believe in me. My mentors my grandparents William and Allene Broughton, Frank and Minnie Bell Singletary and Katherine Sermon. Rev. Shonda Green, Al Akins, Eugenia Mumford, Brandon Giles, Tyronda King, Melanie Thomas-Price, Larceria Willis, Courtney Broughton, Yolanda Hutson, Patricia Bolden, Pastor Debra Ryder, Angela Ayres all of you are true friends and I love you all from the bottom of my heart. Thank you to my Aunts Darlene Seay, Aunt Annie Mae Ford and Aunt Diane Duffy. My wonderful publishing company Jazzy Kitty Greeting Publishing Company aka Jazzy Kitty Publishing. Mt. Zion AME Church, Immanuel House of Praise, Pilgrims Ministry of Deliverance, Dickerson Chapel, Jesus Love Temple, Crossroads of Georgetown, DE.

This writing experience has been phenomenal at the time when I did not know what to write I pushed. Thank you all for your motivational.

I dedicate this book to my succumbed family and friends Evangelist Joy Mifflin, Carol Reid, Paula Hudson, Mark Piper, Grandfather William Broughton, Aunt Helen Burton, Julia Burton, Sebreena Irving…you all were inspirational in my life.

TABLE OF CONTENTS

INTRODUCTION

This workbook is to understand the general principles of business. Overall business principles are used in both for-profit and nonprofit institutions. This workbook provides an overview of these key principles. As you progress through your business education, personal, non-profit, church, and civic organization you will discover that this book is devoted to some of the topics that we take you to the next level in business.

This product will enable the student to learn about personnel management, leadership, and motivational techniques. This workbook is a survey of the functions of business, a comparison of the forms or organizations and methods of administration, and the interdependence of production, distribution and finance in modern business.

For some of you, this workbook may be one of the first that you have taken at the college level. Your future academic success may be influenced by how well you perform. Nothing worth having is easy to acquire. The same is true with your business. Read, take notes, and participate. If you do all of these things, you will discover that business can be successful and it is not difficult, just rigorous.

Course Relevance: The principles learned in this workbook will allow the student to understand the various forms of business domestically and globally. The principles are relevant for everyone, from those entering the workforce for the first time to aspiring entrepreneurs. The workbook also has tips for daily living and your personal finances.

COURSE OBJECTIVES

Upon completion of the workbook the student should be able to:

- Explain the different types of business structures and the benefits of each type
- Define at least three theories of motivation and explain their application
- Understand the basic concepts of interviewing, hiring, training, and employee discipline
- Understand the basics of business entities
- Discuss why businesses exist, how they are structured, and how they are relevant to Federal laws regulations.

- Read & understand a basic income statement or cash flow projections
- Apply the principles of marketing to any business situation
- Know the relevant United States laws concerning hiring, discrimination and disabilities
- Be able to find resources to assist in the enhancement of your personal life or business

Through the student involvement in this workbook, the student will develop and document his/her achievement of their business and personal skills:

- Primary skills developed and documented:
  1. Organization structure/ Time Management
  2. Diversity
  3. Problem Solving
  4. Communication

CHAPTER 1

7 Steps to a Successful Financial Life

7 Steps to a Successful Financial Life

I think we can all agree that **finances play a key role in our lives**. It's the need to provide a quality life for our family that drives most of us to work, and we know that the way we spend our resources directly affects our lifestyle now and down the road.

Money stuff is important.

That is not to say that money is the center of life or that managing the family finances must be an oppressive burden. In fact, financial success is really just a matter of making good choices consistently. Do you know the best path toward achieving your financial goals?

Keep it simple.

Really! In a world dominated by consumerism, credit card commercials and crazy derivative stock options, you will be well-served to take a deep breath and consider what you really want from life. I'm willing to bet that your true priorities fall close to home and close to your heart.

If so, I have some advice that I trust you will value. This isn't earth-shattering and it's really not original. In fact, it is the same advice we have heard from our grandparents our entire lives. It's not complicated, but it sure is effective.

Six Simple Steps for Financial Success

1. Build a basic budget…together.

Okay, so maybe you hate idea of having a budget and counting every penny. Honestly, I don't care how detailed and meticulous you want to be with this. In fact, simple is better. The two key components of a meaningful family budget are: (1) to proactively plan ahead for how you will spend your money and (2) to create it with your spouse. And the real beauty lies in the latter.

You and your spouse must create your budget together and you must agree to follow the same budget, pinkie-swear and spit-shake. When you take this approach, a budget can become a surprisingly valuable tool in your marriage. Real communication is needed to formulate a plan, and real trust is developed when you both stick to it out of respect for your spouse.

2. Work together from a single account.

Do you and your spouse operate with separate checking accounts or a "yours, mine and ours" approach to your family finances? I would strongly encourage you to consider simplifying your life by consolidating everything into a single checking account. Not only will it be easier to keep track of, but you will benefit by shifting your mindset to one of unity with your money. As a bonus, you can expect that the openness and communication required to make a single account a success will carry over and enhance other aspects of your married life.

3. Eliminate your debt.

None of us enjoy sending out those payments to the bank, car finance company or student loan office each month, right? In fact, I think we can all agree that it sucks to have your income spoken for by debt payments before you even receive a paycheck. So, if we all hate the payments, why do so many families have them?

It's a matter of mindset. If you feel like you'll never have anything of value without an accompanying payment book, you're probably right. However, if you are fed up with being normal (i.e., deeply in debt), you can shed the debt and achieve financial freedom. You set the priorities, and you make the decisions that will allow you to dumb the debt. My wife and I paid off over $53,000 in debt in around three years, and I can tell you that it's not easy but it is worth it. And the lack of payments really simplifies your financial life.

4. Stick with simple (and effective) investments.

As a rule, if you don't fully understand something, you should not invest in it. If you chase the latest hot trend and buy what everyone is recommending, you are almost assuring yourself of poor returns. Keep in mind that if thousands of highly-paid professionals spending their entire lives studying the market cannot beat it, neither can you.

Instead, take a simple approach and focus your investing in areas with a long track record of success. Personally, I think it is tough to beat a diversified mix of index mutual funds for retirement investing. They are not sexy or flashy. But they are very effective, low in cost and easy to understand. That's a formula for long-term success.

5. Enjoy the simple things in life. Live within your means.

At the end of the day, it really does come back to living on less than you make. I hope you make a lot of money and love what you do to earn it. However, the critical point here is that you really don't need a ton of money to be financially successful.

The key is contentment. Quit placing your value in material things and trying to maintain a high-cost lifestyle. When you learn to appreciate your family and value the simple pleasures in life, your need to impress the neighbors really does start to fade.

6. Pass it on.

In my opinion, the best part of simplifying your financial life and finding contentment with your lifestyle is the impact it has on your relationship with your spouse and the example it sets for your kids. When you break the cycle of debt dependence and fights about money, you set the stage for financial success for generations to come. You literally have the ability to change the future shape of your family tree.

Were these suggestions brilliant, original and completely unexpected? Of course not. I'd venture to guess that you knew these things, but you may not be living them. The key is to take action.

Invite new success with your money and, most importantly, your life.

1. <u>Create Your Financial Plan</u> and spend some time each week developing and reviewing your plan to make it happen. With every financial transaction, top of mind should be "how does this fit in with my financial goals?"

2. Daily: Take 10 minutes to review your main accounts. Make certain that all charges are accurate and review any purchases you may regret later.

3. Weekly: Review all transactions to help you stay on track with your financial goals

4. Monthly: Review your accounts to make sure that all bills were paid on time or are scheduled to be paid. If the funds aren't there then call the institution to alert them of an expected payment date or work out a payment plan

5. Quarterly: When creating your financial plan, create milestones that benchmark your progress. For example, If your plan is to pay off $10,000 in 12 months then by month 3, you should have $2500 paid off. If that doesn't happen then it's time to readjust the plan and move the goal or play catch up.

6. Write down your financial goals. Goals are the best way to orchestrate success in this area.

7. Set your finances on autopilot. Set up every recurring expense using Bill Pay or via ACH draft.

8. Create a goal statement: My intention is to _____ in order to achieve financial freedom

9. Spend less than you earn

10. Save 20% of income for savings and retirement

11. Pay down non-mortgage debt to less than 15% of income

12. Think long term and spend time in fruitful investments for the future, for example: start a business

13. Read at least 1 personal finance book every month. Keep abreast of emerging financial issues that impact your life.

14. Be mindful of emotional spending. Shopping when you're sad, mad, or depressed often leads to purchases you'll regret later. Address the core issues, as emotional spending only slaps a temporary cover-up on the problem.

15. Spend more time with others who are where you want to be financially. Doing this helps you compare and contrast how you operate with money in comparison to them while helping you

make changes along the way. As my pastor likes to say, seek those who have your solution and get away from those who have your problem.

16. Everyday, day dream and feel what it will be like when you reach your financial goals: debt free, 6-12 months of emergency fund savings-whatever it is-dream about it, talk about, write about it and make it happen.

17. Buy things that will last longer than it takes to finance them. If you finance a TV (you really shouldn't!), then it should last longer than the time it takes to pay it off. This goes for anything, whatever you buy should still be useful 6 months from now.

18. Give back. This can be with your time or money. Spend time time giving back to others less fortunate than yourself.

19. De-clutter your finances. What are some things that you're paying for (magazine subscriptions, extra trips to the makeup counter, techie gadget impulse buys) that leech money you really need to hit your financial goals.

20. Spend time in the future. Leave financial regrets in the past as they took place in order to teach you lessons for the future.

21. Financial problems teach you the life skill of problem solving. If you can dig yourself out of financial ruin, then you'll be surprised as how you face life's other challenges.

22. Research <u>account aggregation</u> tools and commit to monitoring your money on a consistent basis.

23. Every dollar in your budget needs a job. None should be idle and without purpose.

24. The coming financial year won't be perfect. But commit to learning from your mistakes to avoid making them again.

25. With financial freedom comes peace of mind. Work towards this and see how everything else in your life falls into place. Money problems are often the root of other difficulties in life including health and relationships with others.

26. Don't compare your financial situation to others who are in a better position than you are. Remember, like you they had to work to get where they are and if you take anything from their situation, it is that you can one day be financially free yourself.

27. Find peace with your financial past. You may have had some situations that put you in a financial hole but the best part is as long as you're alive today, you have another chance to make things right.

28. Make some hard decisions about your spending habits. How will you <u>Tame Your Achilles Heel</u>? The more insight you have into this area, the better decisions you'll make.

29. Find ways to <u>earn more money</u>. Developing multiple streams of income is key to financial freedom.

30. Your friends won't bail you out of financial ruin if you continue to make bad decisions. If spending money on happy hours, eating out and partying on the weekend take you away from your intended financial goals then it's time to reassess how you spend your money and time.

31. Do the right thing! Avoid "because I deserve it" and "I'm stressed and need retail therapy" purchases. You'll almost always regret them and they do nothing to fix the core issues.

32. Enjoy this time in your life. There are many life lessons to be learned. Spend this time not only about creating a budget but how you got here and the plan to move forward and not fall back.

33. Sell anything that you haven't touched in 6-8 months and pay down debt or plug into savings.

34. Discuss your financial plans for the coming year with your partner or spouse. Make sure you are both on board with goals and how you will address setbacks. Commit to reviewing goals weekly, monthly and quarterly.

35. Start having weekly "family meetings" with each other (couples) and monthly with your children. Part of these meetings will address family finances which discuss spending habits and financial goals.

36. Teach your children about the benefits of entrepreneurship. Instead of another Elmo, <u>PS3</u> or XBox, give them a gumball machine that they will own and operate. This teaches them the inner workings of how a business is run while learning the world of business at a young age.

37. Give children gifts that will last long past the next birthday: create a college fund or add money to a college fund

Learning to live a healthy, happy financial life does not involve one or two magical quick fixes. People who achieve such success do so by adopting an overall healthy financial lifestyle, and maintaining it over the long haul. Can you understand that? Have a look at these concepts, and see if they ring true to you and the lifestyle that your family either already lives, or aspires to live.

Believing in delayed gratification.

Anyone who promises to deliver major, instant *anything* is not being completely honest with you, unless they are selling oatmeal. Instant success, instant beauty, instant weight loss, instant wealth: it's all a bunch of hooey. In life, you generally get what you earn, practice, save for, strive for and put your heart into—over time. What's great about the way of life is that earning these worthwhile things does not have to be complicated or confusing. *Anyone can do it*. And it gives you a helping hand by spelling out the finance terms in plain English, and by outlining simple, stepwise plans you can put in motion immediately in a few weeks or months.

Committing to credit card debt elimination.

You can't live a healthy, happy financial life if you're trapped under a pile of credit card debt. Heck, you can't even get a decent night's sleep. So if you've got more than $1,500 worth of credit card debt that you can't pay off in full, sign up for Consumer Credit Counseling debt and dig yourself out of this hole, once and for all. Stop kidding yourself. Do it now.

Understanding that it takes time to build wealth.

This one is almost the same as the first point, but it's important because it's specifically tied to the concept of wealth. One of the key concepts the author, J.D. Roth, hammers home again and again is that it takes time to build wealth. But if you're patient, consistent and disciplined, anyone can do it. Again, if you're on board it does not have to be difficult, complicated or confusing.

Agreeing that an occasional splurge is imperative.

I'm big on this one. It's sort of a riff on "All work and no play makes Jane a dull girl." It can also cause Jane (and Wendy) to get so tired and fed up with being frugal all the time that they are tempted to let off steam in dangerous and budget-damaging spending sprees. But if you plan for some mini splurges now and then, you can let off steam in smaller, more productive and fun ways.

Valuing education.

This is key on so many levels! You value education by showing interest in what your kids are doing in school, by reading to them early, often and with enthusiasm! You value education by setting up education savings funds when your kids are little. You value education by taking your kids to the zoo, the park, the museum, the arboretum, to the city, your backyard, down the street anywhere but the mall and by showing them things, asking them their opinions and then just listening to what they have to say. Doing these things places a premium on education. It pays off not just in your own kids, but also for generations to come, and in the sort of wealth that both includes and transcends dollars.

Prioritizing health.

You don't sit on the couch, watch reruns of The Office (which I admit is a great show) and eat a pack of Little Debbie Snack Cakes every day. You know it would be irresponsible to yourself, your kids, and to the rest of us, who pitch in to pay for the pool of health care that many of us are in together. No, you don't do that. You work out when you can, eat responsibly, and put healthy foods in front of your kids as often as possible. Sometimes you even take the stairs. Nicely done! So why is prioritizing health on a finance website? First, because the less you take care of yourself physically, the more you tend to rack up health care expenses, now and in the future. And second, because I'm a Mom, remember?

These are key components to a healthy, happy financial lifestyle. If these ring true to you, I urge try being financially stable. In this book, you'll get to learn all sorts of savvy insider tips, such as how to save money at club stores by avoiding this common club store pricing tactic, from a former corporate marketing insider (me)!

You'll get:

- Sound financial wisdom

- Stepwise instructions on how to meet your financial goals

- A swift kick in the hind to move forward

  Everyone needs a bit of encouragement from time to time. Thankfully we have the Bible as our ultimate source of encouragement! Even in the midst of the "financial crisis" that we are in the middle of, we can remain hopeful and encouraged if we keep trusting in God.

  Here are some scriptures of encouragement for your finances.

"And my God will meet all your needs according to his glorious riches in Christ Jesus." – *Phil 4:19*

Notice the above verse says "ALL." It doesn't say "some" or "most," but it says that He will meet all of our needs. It doesn't say how He will meet our needs and I have found from experience the way He does it is often not what I expected. But the bottom line is that God is faithful and He does what He promises.

10 of my favorite encouraging bible verses

- "These things I have spoken to you, so that in Me you may have peace. In the world you have tribulation, but take courage; I have overcome the world." *John 16:33*

- God is our refuge and strength, a very present help in trouble. Therefore we will not fear, though the earth should change and though the mountains slip into the heart of the sea; though its waters roar and foam, though the mountains quake at its swelling pride. Selah. The LORD of hosts is with us; the God of Jacob is our stronghold. Selah. *Psalm 46:1-3,7*

- 'Do not fear, for I am with you; do not anxiously look about you, for I am your God. I will strengthen you, surely I will help you, surely I will uphold you with My righteous right hand.' *Isaiah 41:10*

- For God did not give us a spirit of timidity (of cowardice, of craven and cringing and fawning fear), but [He has given us a spirit] of power and of love and of calm and well-balanced mind and discipline and self-control. *2 Tim 1:7 (AMP)*

- I have set the Lord continually before me; because He is at my right hand, I shall not be moved. *Psalm 16:8 (AMP)*

- Cast your burden on the Lord [releasing the weight of it] and He will sustain you; He will never allow the [consistently] righteous to be moved (made to slip, fall, or fail). *Psalm 55:22 (AMP)*

- He only is my Rock and my Salvation; He is my Defense and my Fortress, I shall not be moved. *Psalm 62:6 (AMP)*

- Casting the whole of your care [all your anxieties, all your worries, all your concerns, once and for all] on Him, for He cares for you affectionately and cares about you watchfully. *1 Peter 5:7 (AMP)*

- The Lord is good, a Strength and Stronghold in the day of trouble; He knows (recognizes, has knowledge of, and understands) those who take refuge and trust in Him. *Nahum 1:7 (AMP)*

- "The steadfast of mind You will keep in perfect peace, Because he trusts in You. *Isaiah 26:3*

Surveys have shown that money is one of the main causes of stress. The recession increased money woes for many of us - playing up our fears of joblessness or putting more pressure on us to make ends meet on a smaller budget. Although those in their twenties are known to struggle with uncertainty, personal finance is something that the younger generation can immediately start to take control of. Kimberly Palmer, author of Generation Earn and personal finance expert for U.S. News and World Report, shares several secrets to how young professionals can take a positive approach to becoming financially secure. Here are 10 tips from her new book:

- **Don't skimp on what makes you happy:** Whether it's a new pair of fall boots or daily java, the quickest way to destroy your budget is to make it impossible to follow. That's why you should cut the costs that don't matter to you, which might mean cooking more meals at home or living in a smaller apartment, while splurging (guilt-free) on the ones that do.

- **That includes investing in your career:** Since your profession is what has the potential to make you money, that's the last place you want to cut costs. So whether it's time to revamp your office wardrobe, take a career advancement course, or work with a coach, make the investment now so you can see the pay-off later.

- **Track your money:** Starting now, write down everything you spend money on for the next two weeks. You might discover that you're letting small costs stress you out while ignoring the bigger bank account leaks.

- **Enforce the $100 cut-off:** For bigger purchases, there's almost always wiggle room on the price. So before buying anything over $100, be sure to research your options first by hunting around online, checking comparison sites such as PriceGrabber.com, and even negotiating with sales clerks.

- **Get a second job:** Consider taking on a freelance assignment or two. The average worker now has 10 different jobs before age 36, which means we need to think of ourselves as entrepreneurs, and always be on the lookout for new opportunities.

- **Plunge into that stock market:** Yes, investing can be a scary thing. But it's also the best way to earn money over the long-term, so don't wait until you feel like you have"extra" money before learning how to invest in index funds and other low-cost options. If you have access to a retirement account, such as a 401(k), through your job, then start there.

- **Plan on funding your own retirement:** The days of pensions and a fully-funded Social Security trust fund will soon be over. That means we have to fund much of our retirements on our own. There's only one way to do that - saving a lot, and starting as soon as possible. According to the Transamerica Center for Retirement, single women, on average, need to have saved $500,000 by the time they retire.

- **Take baby steps:** The easiest way to get started is to begin by saving just two percent of your income. Then, slowly increase that to four percent and higher. Soon, you'll be funneling away 20 percent into your retirement account and headed toward blissed-out golden years.

- **Simplify:** Are there ways you could simplify your life while also enjoying it more? Maybe you'd rather watch less television and bike to work instead of driving. Blogs on the pursuit of simplicity, such as smallnotebook.org, can provide inspiration.

- **Think like a celebrity:** Ever notice how all the biggest names join up with good causes or even launch their own charities? Wyclef Jean, Michael Phelps, and Ashton Kutcher are just a few of the celebs who have donated their time and money to causes they believe in. While they have access to more resources than the rest of us, we can often make similar moves on a smaller scale. If you've noticed an unmet need in your community, think of what you could do to help. Perhaps getting together with friends to raise money would let you spend more time together while also giving back.

- A great way to ensure you have enough money to spend from that which you earn every month is to know your priorities. You need to understand that you can't get everything you see and that money shouldn't just be spent as you have it. You need to plan you"impulse buying."

- What is it that you really need? What is it you can't do without? Or as an entrepreneur r spending carefully, and this also means you have to be careful about, what will help increase the chances of your business succeeding? These are questions you should always ask yourself.

- Once you know which things are the most important to get in a given month, put them on the top of your list of what to get and try as much as you can to weed out those things that are less important.

Focus on Generating More Income Instead of Reducing Your Debt

It's good not to have debt. It's good to look for ways to reduce your debt. And, it's even good to learn as much as you can regularly on being debt free. But the fact is, how can you be debt free when you have very little to live on? Instead of thinking always about ways to be debt free, ways to plan your income and things like that why not give more attention to earning more money? This can be in various forms, which can include <u>selling part of your time for money</u>, <u>working on creating passive income streams</u>, leveraging the power of others who have the money you need and <u>learning about other pretty cool ways to increase your income</u>.

It is good to manage, but it is better to create. It will be easier for you to live a debt free life if you have enough money to spend than if you only make a fraction of what you should be making.

Have a Monthly Spending Limit

If only everybody in debt could have a monthly spending limit, it would have been very difficult for them to get into debt in the first place. The main reason for getting into debt is living on something other than ours, and this can easily be prevented if we could learn to manage what we have.

Always ensure you limit your spending every month as much as you can, which means you should NEVER spend more than you earn in any given month. I will personally suggest that you do your best not to spend more than 70% of your personal earnings in a single month because by so doing you will easily prevent yourself from going into debt while at the same time having enough to save.

As you can see, lot of things have simplified our lives, and one such thing is our credit card, but little do we know that things like our credit cards are simplifying our present and are compounding our future. Credit cards are attractive, in fact, they are the norm but the truth is we can do without them. It usually seems like your credit card is always there to help when you are in need of something and just can't afford it but the question is *why do you even need what you can't afford in the first place?*

Our credit cards come with a lot of hidden charges, they make it easy for us to buy things we don't need and the end result of this is us going into debt at the very first chance possible. Instead of having a credit card, why not restrict yourself to buying only what you can afford and why not save what you'll otherwise be paying as interest?

If you want a card at all means, maybe to pay for online purchases and do some other related things, why not get a debit card that restricts you to spending the amount you have. By having this you will be sure you owe nobody and you will be able to avoid hidden charges at all cost. We must trust God to maximize the moment. Spend only what you can pay for in cash!

CHAPTER 2

Is Your Life Complete?

When we talk about living a complete life, what do we mean? Are we talking about simply achieving goals as a way to show accomplishments? Not exactly, a complete life means that you live a life that is fulfilled and full of happiness.

Goals are an important part of it, but so are personal and professional relations, passions and desires. For almost everyone, living a complete life is an ongoing process – every day we take steps or perform tasks that help us achieve the goals and desires we have set forth in our life.

It's very easy to live life to go through the motions without living fulfilled. Far too many of us are getting up every day and we don't have a passion or purpose in what we do. We've lost track of our life goals and are not sure how to get back on the path towards living a fulfilled life.

So how do we get back on track in our lives? Or if we already are on track, what are some of the tips that can help keep us on track? I've compiled a list of 5 areas that you can focus on that can help you achieve living a fulfilled and complete life.

1. **Turn Your Desires and Wants into Goals**

    We all have **desires and wants** in our life. For some of us it can be a desire to be able to retire early, for others we may have a want to get the latest BMW. For many people they have a desire to make sure that they leave behind a legacy of doing well in both their personal and professional lives.

    In order to achieve your wants and desires, set up goals for yourself. In fact, many people find that by having goals and milestones to achieving that goal that they have the motivating power to actually make it happen. Setting up goals gives you the purpose for getting up in the morning and helps fuel the drive to succeed. Make sure your goals are achievable by breaking them down into smaller steps. Then celebrate each time you achieve one of the steps towards the larger goal!

2. **Turn Your Goals into Habits**

    Now that you have defined your goals, or better yet you have achieved them, don't step there! Turn those goals into habits. If your goal was to finish your college education then make it a habit make education a part of your everyday life by always learning and doing. If your goal was to get rid of the clutter in your life then make sure you don't stop once you have achieved it or else the clutter will find its way back into your life!

    Habits help us continually achieve goals and even help take small goals and transform them into larger ones. For instance, if you have achieved your goal of reducing your energy and water usage help others see the benefits of doing so as well expand your goal by making it your habit! People learn by seeing others do.

3. **Track Your Progress and Celebrate Your Accomplishments**

    If you remember, I said that in order to make your goals achievable to break them down into smaller steps and celebrate each step as you achieve it. It's important that we recognize the progress we make in our lives and that our friends and family make in theirs. It's positive reinforcement and it is one of the most crucial ingredients in leading a happy, fulfilled life.

    Celebrate accomplishments and use the momentum from achieving that milestone as the catalyst to propel you towards the next milestone! You will find that soon you have developed a positive self-feeding cycle in your life and you will be able to achieve anything you put your mind to!

4. **Watch Out For the Negatives**

    How many of us limit ourselves by listening to old, outdated and just plain wrong advice and conventions? When people tell you that you can't do something because you haven't done X or Y first, just smile and tell them "Thanks, but I think I'll give it a shot!" **Never limit yourself or your beliefs**.

It seems that in life people are always more apt to listen to those who want to spread the negative emotions and thoughts around than they are those who want to spread around the message of "Yes you can!" Learn how to overcome those who want to be held back by old, outdated beliefs and propel yourself forward knowing that you can do something if you work hard at it.

Bill Gates, the founder of Microsoft, didn't believe in the old belief at the time that IBM didn't do business with small companies and look at where he is now!

5. **Keep Your Mind Open Change**

We should always make sure that we have an open mind and learn that change happens and sometimes we need to modify our desires or goals. This doesn't mean you should give up on something because you think it is too hard to achieve, but rather you should be open for new ways of achieving that goal or modifying the goal to take advantage of advanced in technology, science and the world around us.

Successful people know that change is part of life and that change does not, as many people believe, happen suddenly but rather is a gradual process that takes place every minute of the day. By being aware of the change that happens around them they can better focus their goals and desires to take advantage of change instead of being surprised by it.

Are you preparing to bring fulfillment to your life? Use this list as guide then watch as change starts to happen around you. People will notice when you change your attitude and outlook, and when they do it is almost viral they begin to change theirs as well! Before you know it, not only are you living a full, complete life but you also were the catalyst for others to find fulfillment in their lives as well!

Educate Yourself

There are countless ways to prevent yourself from getting into debt but the best thing you can do is educate yourself. There is a lot of free advice online in the form of blog posts, online articles, newsletters and the likes. Ensure you subscribe to reliable blogs and newsletters. Ensure you invest your money and time into reading highly informative books on money management.

You might not have a million dollars, and you might not be able to get the best financial planner or advisor but the little information you can read on many blogs and books will save you a fortune!

52 Tips for Happiness and Productivity

Try rising early. It's not for everyone, I'll admit. It may not be for you. But I've found it to be an amazing change in my life. It has made the start of my days much more positive, and I now have time for writing, exercise, and silent contemplation. This is both a happiness and productivity tip. Doing less will make you happier, because your life won't be so hectic and filled with stress. You will have time for things that give you pleasure, for the loved ones in your life, for life itself. It's also a productivity tip: if you focus on the essential tasks, the big ones, the ones that will give you the most return for your time, and eliminate the rest, you will actually be more productive. You'll get fewer tasks done, but you will be more effective.

Slow down. By doing less, you can actually get more done, even if you work more slowly. And when you're not working, you should definitely try switching to slow mode. Drive slower (it is so much more relaxing), walk slower, eat slower.

Practice patience. If you easily lose your temper, you can become more patient with these tips. Once you've developed this skill (and it's a skill, like everything else, not an unchangeable inborn trait), your life will become much saner and you will be much happier.

Practice compassion. This may be the most important tip of all, in my opinion. If you were to choose any of these, I would choose this one. The first part of compassion is empathy and this ability to understand how others feel can be developed through practice. Start by imagining the suffering of a loved one. Understand their pain, the emotions they go through, and why they would react the way they would. By doing this exercise a number of times, you are developing a skill that can be applied to others for every person you see, try to understand what they are going through. Try to learn and understand more about their background, and why they react the way they do. Once you've developed this invaluable skill, learn the other half of compassion acting on your understanding, and helping others, alleviating their suffering, acting with kindness. This one thing can bring true happiness to your life, and the lives of those around you.

Find your passion. Another indispensable tip. This might be the second on my list of priorities. Find something you love to do, and your life will become immensely improved. You will love your work, the thing that you spend 40 hours (or more) a week doing. You will become more productive, procrastinate less, be less stressed. You will produce something you are proud of, and happy about.

Lose weight. This only applies, of course, if you are overweight. But losing your extra fat (and when I say lose weight, I mean lose fat), decreases your health risks obviously, makes you look better, and in general is very likely to increase your happiness about yourself. I actually recommend that you learn to be comfortable and happy with how you look now, and not feel negative about yourself even if you are overweight. However, I've found that losing weight (at least for me) is a great way to feel better about your body. Do not make this an unhealthy obsession, however lose weight gradually, and enjoy the process.

Exercise. Make this a daily habit. Exercise not only helps you lose weight, but for me, it's made me feel so much better. I actually enjoy exercise now. It's a time of contemplation for me, and I feel so much better about myself afterwards..

Eat healthy. I don't recommend dieting. It's too restrictive and you usually fall off it at some point. I do recommend changes to your diet, however — ones you make gradually, and that can be sustained for life. It not only helps lose weight, but really, once you start eating healthier, it is actually much more enjoyable.

Meditate. Okay, you might be like me — not into New-Age stuff. But meditation can actually be a very simple method for relaxing, for bringing calm, for returning yourself to sanity, for contemplation.

Get organized. This one's not necessary. You could go through life wonderfully messy, searching for stuff, enjoying the search. But I've tried disorganized, and I've tried organized. The second is much more enjoyable to me.

Think positive. Another one of the most important tips on this list, thinking positive — as cliche as it might sound is one of the single best changes you can make in your life that will lead to so many more positive tips. It makes everything else on this list possible.

Simplify your finances. Cut down on the number of accounts you have, cut down on your credit cards, spend less, reduce your bills. Simplifying your finances greatly reduces your stress. **Simplify your life**. Another of my top tips. I've greatly simplified my life, in many ways, and I can say that having less stuff in my life, and less to do, has greatly increased my enjoyment of life. De-clutter, simplify your commitments, simplify your work space, simplify your wardrobe, simplify your rooms.

Accept what you have. The problem with many of us is that we always think that we'll be happy when we reach a certain destination , when we get a certain job, or retire, or get our dream house. Unfortunately, it takes a while before you get there, and when you get there, you might have a new destination in mind. Instead, try being happy with where you are, with who you are, and what you have. To do that, instead of comparing what you have with other people, or with what you want, compare yourself those who have less, with those who are going through tragedy, with those who are struggling. You will see that you actually are extremely blessed. And this can lead to more happiness with your current situation.

Envision your ultimate life. What would your ultimate life be like? Where would you live, what would you do, what would you do with your days? Come up with a clear picture of this, and write it down. Now, one step at a time, make it come true. Some ways of doing that follow.

Set long-term goals. Your vision of your ultimate life will help you come up with long-term goals. Of those goals, pick one to accomplish within the next year, and really focus on that. Now, pick one medium-term goal to achieve in the next few months that will get you further toward your longer-term goal. Now decide what you can do this week, and today, to get you to your medium-term goal. Just choose one thing at a time, focus on it, make it happen, and then choose the next thing to focus on.

Review goals. Setting goals is important, but the key to making them a reality is actually reviewing them (at least monthly, but weekly is better) and taking action steps to make them come true. Again, focus on one at a time, and really focus on them..

Life mission. Related to envisioning your ultimate life, but different — it's important that you think about how you would like to be remembered when you die — so you can start living the life that leads to that now. Live with purpose in life, and wake up every day with that purpose in mind.

Plan your big tasks for week and day. Give purpose to your day by determining the three most important things you can do with your day, and making those a priority. Do the same thing with your week to increase your productivity: pick out the big tasks you'd like to accomplish this week, and schedule those first.

Maintain focus. One important key to achieving your goals is to maintain focus on them. To do this, again, it's important that you select one goal at a time. This will prevent your focus from spreading too thin. It's also important that you give yourself constant reminders of your goal, so you don't lose that focus. Put up a poster of your current goal, or print it out and put it out somewhere visible, and send yourself emailed reminders. However you do it, find a way to maintain a laser-sharp focus, and the goal will come true.

Enjoy the journey. Goals are important, but not at the expense of happiness now. It's important to maintain a balance between going where you want to go, and being happy as you go there. It's easy to forget that, so be sure to remind yourself of this little, but important, tip as you make your journey.

Create a morning and evening routine. These are two great ways to add structure to your day, make sure you review your goals and log your progress, and get your day off to a great start. An evening routine, for example, could be a great way not only to wind down from a long day and review how your day went, but to prepare yourself for your next day so the morning isn't so hectic. Your morning routine is great way to greet the day, to get some exercise or meditation or quiet contemplation, or to get some writing or other work done.

Develop intimate relationships. It's great to have a special someone, of course, but intimate relationships could be found with anyone around you. If you have a significant other, be sure to spend time each day and each week with that person, to work on your relationship and communicate and continue to bond. But if you don't, there's no need to despair (if in fact you are)...intimate relationships can be developed with friends, other family members, kids, roommates, classmate, co-workers. Every single person we meet is a fellow human being, with the same desires for happiness, for food and shelter, for an intimate connection. Find that common thread, be open and sincere, find out more about each other, understand each other, and give love. This can be one of the most important things you do.

Eliminate debt. Financially, this is a huge way to relieve stress and make you feel much more secure. I suggest that you get rid of your credit cards (if you have a problem with credit card debt or impulse spending) and create a snowball plan for yourself. It may take a couple of years, but you can get out of debt.

Enjoy the simple pleasures. You can find these everywhere. Food (I love berries!), sunsets, sand between your toes, fresh-cut grass, playing with your child, a good book and a warm bed, dancing in the rain, your favorite music. You could probably make a list of 20 simple pleasures right now, things you enjoy that you could find every day. Sprinkle those little pleasures throughout your day. It makes the journey much more enjoyable.

Empty your inbox and clear your desk. This might take a little while to do at first, but once you've emptied your inbox and cleared off your desk, it doesn't take long to keep them clear from then on. It's a simple habit that's vastly rewarding. I get an inordinate amount of pleasure from having a clean desk. I recommend you give it a try.

Build an emergency fund. This is standard-issue financial advice, I know…and yet it is extremely important. I cannot stress how important it is to have at least a tiny emergency fund in the bank. You often hear that you should have six months saved up. Don't be intimidated by that. Start out with just a hundred dollars if you can. Cut back on a few things. Then build it up, every payday. Once you have, let's say, $1,000, it will make a huge difference in your life. It's not much, and you should still add to it every paycheck, but at least now you're not living paycheck-to-paycheck, and if an unexpected emergency comes up you can pay for it, rather than not paying other bills and falling behind. It's a simple step, but it will mean a lot.

Keep a journal. This is not one of the more important tips, but I can attest that it's rewarding. I, for one, have a bad long-term memory, and by writing things down, I can look back and remember what happened a month ago. I just started this a couple months ago, actually, but it's been awesome. I started an online journal, something I call the one-sentence journal, and my goal is to just write one sentence a day. Sometimes I write two or three, but the idea is the same — just get one or two things down that happened that day, so I can always look back on it later.

Use the power of others. Achieving your goals can be difficult, but using the power of others makes it much more likely to happen. For example, put positive public pressure on yourself by announcing your goal on your blog. Or join an online forum, or a group in your neighborhood, that you can count on for support. I have a mailing list for the May Challenge here on Zen Habits, for example, and our group has helped me stick to my goal of daily exercise even when I started to falter and the rest of the group can tell you they've experienced similar success because of the positive power of the group.

Read, and read to your kids. I read all the time. It's one of my favorite things to do in the world. I love to curl up with a good novel (or even a trashy one) and I can waste away an afternoon with a book. And I'm passing on my love of reading to my kids, by reading to them every day. I love spending time with them this way, and we all enjoy the stories we share together through books.

Limit your information intake. In our lives today, we get a tremendous amount of information through email, blog feeds, reading websites, paperwork, memos, newspapers, magazines, television, DVDs, radio, mobile phones and Blackberries. Not only can this be overwhelming, but it can be distracting and can fill up your life until you have no time for more important things. Get control over your information intake, and to simplify your life

Create simple systems. Once you've simplified your life, the way to keep it simple is by creating systems for everything you do regularly. Create an efficient system for laundry, mail and paperwork, errands, your workflow. Anything, really

Take time to decompress after stress. There will inevitably be times in your life when you go through high stress. Perhaps several times a week. To maintain your sanity, you need to find ways to decompress. **Be present**. Time can go by extremely quickly. Before you know it, your life has passed you by. Your kids are grown and your youth is gone. Don't let your life slip by — enjoy it while it's here. Instead of dwelling in the past or thinking about the future, practice being in the here and now. **Develop equanimity**. Keep your sanity through all the challenges that life throws at you. Rude drivers, irritating co-workers, mean commenters on your blog, inconsiderate family members.

Spend time with family and loved ones. One of the things that can lead to the greatest happiness, make this a priority every week, every day. Clear off as much time as possible to spend with those you love, and truly enjoy those times. Be present as you do it — don't think about work or your blog or what you need to do.

Pick yourself up when you're down. There will always be times in our lives when we get a little down, even depressed. Take action to get yourself out of your slump.

Don't compare yourself to others. This is hard to do, but it can be a great way to accept who you are and what you have. Whenever you find yourself comparing yourself to a co-worker, a friend, or someone famous (those models on magazines with amazing abs), stop. And realize that you are different, with different strengths. Take a minute to appreciate all the good things about yourself, and to be grateful for all the blessings in your life.

Focus on benefits, not difficulties. If you find yourself struggling to do something, or procrastinating, stop thinking about how hard something is, or why you don't want to do it. Focus instead on what benefits it will have for you, what opportunities it will create — the good things about it. By changing the way you see things, you can change how you feel about them and make it easier to get things done.

Be romantic. If you have that special someone, find little ways to be romantic. It can do wonders to keep your relationship alive and fresh. It doesn't take tons of money, either.

Lose arguments. I know someone who just celebrated his 50th anniversary, and I asked him for his secret to a long and happy marriage. He told me, that if I ever get into an argument with my wife, to just shut up. What he meant, I think, is that I shouldn't try to be right in every argument. I think this is a reminder many of us need, not just the married ones. But instead of just giving up the argument, instead of trying to be right, instead seek to understand. Really try to understand the other person's position, to see it from their point of view. This little tip can lead to much happiness.

Get into the flow. This is both a happiness and productivity tip. Flow is the term for the state we enter when we are completely focused on the work or task before us. We are so immersed in our task that we lose track of time. Having work and leisure that gets you in this state of flow will almost undoubtedly lead to happiness. People find greatest enjoyment not when they're passively mindless, but when they're absorbed in a mindful challenge. Get into that flow by first doing something you are passionate about, and second by eliminating all distractions and really focusing on the task before you.

Single-task. I don't believe in multi-tasking, at least not on a day-to-day basis. Instead, focus on one task at a time. This leads to greater productivity and less stress. You can't go wrong with that kind of combination.

Be frugal. This is a habit, rather than a goal. It is a way of living, a different mindset, and the best way to live within your means. It doesn't mean being cheap or forsaking pleasure, but it does mean finding less expensive ways to do things, learning to live with less (and be happier in the process), and controlling impulse spending.

Start small and slow. Regular Zen Habits readers know that I advocate starting slow with any goal or habit change, and starting with a small goal rather than a big one. Why small? Because it's something you are sure to achieve — and once you do achieve it, you can use that success to push you to further success. It's a simple technique, but it really works. Start slow when you start exercise, or other similar activities. There's no need to rush it in the beginning, to overdo it. You have the rest of your life!

Learn to deal with detractors. We all face detractors in our lives. They are the naysayers who, even if they are well-intentioned, will make us feel unworthy, or that you cannot achieve a goal. They will tease or be negative. In order to achieve your goals, you need to learn how to deal with these detractors and overcome this common obstacle..

Go outdoors. These days, too many of us spend so much of our time indoors, especially if our jobs and our ways of having fun are all online. Our kids are often just as bad or worse, with so many ways to watch TV, surf the internet or play video games. Get them and yourself outdoors, appreciate nature, the beauty of the world around us, and the fun of physical activity. **Retire early**. This isn't a sure way to become happy — you can retire and be bored out of your mind and unhappy — but it's surely a cool goal. And if you do something meaningful with your life, such as volunteer and help others, it can be a way to be really happy. It's not an easy goal, either, but you can retire early by cutting back on your living expenses, increasing your income, and investing the difference. The more you can do of all three, the fast you'll retire. And that's a truly liberating idea.

Savor the little things. Sure, the big things can bring big pleasure, but there are so many more little things in our lives. Savor them when they come up. It's a way of practicing being present — stop and notice what you're doing right now, what's around you. And take time to enjoy it.

Be lazy. There's a time to be productive, and there's a time to be plain ol' lazy. I like the latter, and do it every chance I get. Does that make me a lazy person? Probably not, but even if it does, I don't care. It makes me happy, and the kids love being lazy with me.

Help others. While finding pleasure in life is one way to be happy, doing something that is more than you, that helps others to be happy or to suffer less, is even more rewarding. I suggest you find a good cause or two and volunteer some of your time. You don't have to commit to big chunks of your life, but just volunteer for a couple of hours. All of us can find a couple of hours in a week or a month. If you do this, you will find out how tremendously happy this will make you. You might even become addicted.

Seek Strength

1 Chronicles 16:11 *Seek the LORD and his strength; seek his presence continually!*

Strength Through Christ

Philippians 4:13 *I can do all things through him who strengthens me.*

Not Of Fear

2 Timothy 1:7 *for God gave us a spirit not of fear but of power and love and self-control.*

Keep Doing Good

2 Thessalonians 3:13 *As for you, brothers, do not grow weary in doing good.*

Galatians 6:9 *And let us not grow weary of doing good, for in due season we will reap, if we do not give up.*

Hope

Romans 12:12 *Rejoice in hope, be patient in tribulation, be constant in prayer.*

Jeremiah 29:11 *For I know the plans I have for you, declares the LORD, plans for welfare and not for evil, to give you a future and a hope.*

Peace

Romans 8:6 *For to set the mind on the flesh is death, but to set the mind on the Spirit is life and peace.*

Patience

1 Thessalonians 5:14 *And we urge you, brothers, admonish the idle encourage the fainthearted, help the weak, be patient with them all.*

Joyful Heart

Proverbs 17:22 *A joyful heart is good medicine, But a crushed spirit dries up the bones.*

The Top 100 Christian Financial Websites

Crown.org – The Crown Financial website has hundreds of articles sorted by topic and has lots of other goodies and resources.

eChristianFinance.com – A good place to find some good articles about Christian finances and stewardship. They also have a bunch of tools and worksheets as well.

Generousgiving.org – This site is just loaded with information. There are tons of videos, audio interviews, articles, etc.

Masteryourmoney.com – Ron Blue's site that has tons of free videos answering common financial questions. Seriously, I think they have a video answer to every question you could have about your money.

Moralmoney.com – MoralMoney is focused on helping Christians make investment decisions that line up with their beliefs. They have a free newsletter and a free stock-screening tool that will help you decide if a company is worthy of your investment dollars.

The Top Christian Blogs

Biblemoneymatters.com – Bible Money Matters is a blog that was launched in February of 2008 as a place for Pete to put down his thoughts on matters of his Christian faith and how it affects his finances. Pete writes really good content and I encourage you to check it out.

Borrowfromnone.com – This blog is written by John and the name is based off the wonderful verse in Deut 28:12 – "that you will lend to many nations, but will borrow from none." While John only gets to update it a couple times a week, he is a great writer and always has good things to say.

Centsablemomma.com – Corrie is a momma who writes this mom-blog that focuses on frugality and couponing. If you are looking to learn more about couponing, this would be a good site to check out.

Christianfinanceblog.com – Henry started this blog a couple of years ago and has been faithful to pass along biblical revelation as he uncovers it. He often reminds readers of scriptures relevant to our finances.

ChristianMoneyMountain.com – Travis started this blog a couple just a couple months ago and I have been impressed with the quality of articles he has on it. He tends to post every other day and has a good mix of articles.

Crackerjackgreenback.com – A fairly new blog written by Paul who is a Christian Financial Planner. He writes about prudent ways to handle your money and often discusses how scriptures should affect our decisions.

Freemoneyfinance.com – This blog has been around for years and puts out more content than any blog I know. I think he posts about 7 times a day and every sunday FMF writes about the Bible and Money.

Gatherlittlebylittle.com – This blog is written by "Gibble" and he started right around the time I started ChristianPF. The site was birthed out of a very challenging time in his life, but he says, and I agree, that "it's a terrible place to be when you are there, but you learn more than you ever thought possible." The blog is frequently updated and always has interesting content.

Jayperoni.com – I have known Jay for a few months now and have enjoyed his no-holds-barred writing on his blog. He is an author and investment professional and has a passion to help Christians invest according to their beliefs. He also has a very well done radio show that you can listen to on his site as well.

Kingdomfirstmom.com – As the name suggests this is a mom-blog. Alyssa puts it best when she says her mission is to, "to save more and give more, one coupon at a time."

Rcvogler.com – Another Bob writes this site that is primarily focused on finances. He does a good job of finding useful articles from the corners of the web...

Richchristianpoorchristian.com – This is an encouraging and motivating blog written by Pastor Larry Jones. He writes a lot about stewardship, personal motivation and success.

Sensiblesteward.com – This blog is run by another Dave Ramsey fan and has been going for a couple years now. As the name suggests it is geared towards becoming the best stewards we can with what we've been given.

Toddcolucy.com – Todd is a church CPA who has been writing his blog for almost 3 years. He says the blog is his creative outlet. He typically posts about twice a week and often writes quick nuggets of wisdom from his personal experiences.

Wealthfromthebible.com – CoolHappyGuy writes this blog and I wish I could get him to update it more! He writes scripture-packed thought-provoking articles that provide some helpful insight about biblical money management.

God is there for you and willing to show Himself strong on your behalf.

CHAPTER 3

From Brokenness to Wholeness/A Check List to Financial Freedom

From Brokenness to Wholeness

Someone out there may be asking what does brokenness have to do with finances, success and your purpose. It has a great deal to due with the total you. Today, I want to talk with you about taking the journey from brokenness to wholeness. Millions of people are **broken hearted** by circumstances such as finances, poor relationships with others, sinfulness, and physical testing. Throughout His ministry on earth, Jesus met people in desperate need of help. Perhaps you are broken in spirit. Instead of being broken, you want to be made whole.

Brokenness Hurts!

Brokenness hurts! Nothing hurts more than a broken heart. Suddenly you feel alone and isolated. You search for answers, but it seems there are none. Even when a possible answer can be found, it seems that it never heals a broken heart. The pain that some people endure is indescribable.

Brokenness can take many forms. It may include insignificance, emptiness, excessive anxiety, bitterness, depression, addictions, persistent shame, obsessive thoughts, compulsive behaviors, and even perfectionism. People who suffer from perfectionism simply cannot live up to their own expectations.

Many people are enduring broken relationships. Dr. Richard Swenson in his book entitled "A Minute of Margin" states: "Broken relationships are a razor across the artery of the spirit. Stemming the hemorrhage and binding the wound should be done as quickly as possible. Yet all too often it takes months or years. And sometimes the bleeding never stops."

Many Try Substitutes

All over the world people attempt to overcome pain by filling their lives with substitutes. These substitutes include alcohol, drugs, sex, material things, and even work. The main idea is to numb the pain with something else. Usually people hope to avoid pain with these substitutes. However, most of these substitutes only increase feelings of brokenness, hopelessness, and lead to lower self-esteem. Individuals have known to become suicidal due to finances.

If we attempt to lift ourselves out of brokenness and become whole without turning to God, we will fail. We may, to be sure, be able to improve our lot in life, but complete wholeness is not possible. We must turn to our creator for help. He alone has the complete answer for us. Given this, let us begin our search for God, He is the King of mending a broken heart. Indeed, because of His love, He is searching for us! He wants us to respond.

Wholeness Through Christ

Wholeness is what we want. We want to be whole in body, soul, and spirit, but we cannot be whole on our own. In order to be whole, we have to be reconciled to God through Christ. Christ died for our sins upon the cross. As we believe in Him and follow His teachings, He can help us deal with our brokenness.

According to John 10:10, Jesus said: "I came that they might have life, and might have it abundantly." Here, Jesus states His goal. He wants us to have abundant life. This abundant life does not always shield us from brokenness, but it will help us through the dark seasons and give us victory. The Psalmist (147:3) says, "He heals the brokenhearted, and binds up their wounds." Jesus is always present to treat our wounds and heal our suffering hearts. He will give us abundant life!

So to overcome our brokenness we must realize that we have to be healed by a power greater than ourselves. If we look only to ourselves, we will be not be able to make the journey from brokenness to wholeness. Jesus will not impose His healing upon us. We must make the decision to turn to Him for healing.

God With Us

Even in times of great testing, God is with us. Psalm 34:18 says, "The Lord is near to the broken-hearted, and saves those who are crushed in spirit." This assertion gives us great hope. Even the darkest hours can be moments of peak fellowship with the eternal God. Our Lord will heal our crushed hearts.

Swenson writes about the healing of broken relationships. He states: "Although there is no formula, there are principles. It helps to bring God close through our brokenness. And it helps to accept God's grace through our humility." Through brokenness and humility, with God near, our broken relationships can be healed. As Swenson says, "Warring individuals who have done battle for years can erase all antagonism in a matter of minutes."

Moreover, when people have experienced brokenness, they often minister more effectively. People who have been healed from brokenness can identify with those who are broken. We do not seek to be broken, but when we are, God can use it for His glory.

The Process of Brokenness

Through adversity, God *targets* the areas of self-will in our lives. He wants to break the attitudes that do not honor Him such as self-righteousness, self-reliance, and self-centeredness. The result is that He fills our lives with spiritual fruit (Gal. 5:22-23). Examples: Moses was broken in the desert. He spent 40 years learning to obey the Lord, before God used him to free Israel from Egyptian bondage. The apostle Paul's "thorn in the flesh" kept him from exalting himself, despite his impressive credentials (2 Cor. 12:7). Jesus corrected Peter's pride many times (Matt. 14:24-31; Matt. 16:21-23; Matt. 26:33-35; Luke 22:54-62; John 13:5-10; John 18:1-11) so that the apostle could lead the church (Acts 2:14-47).

We are only as useful to God as we are obedient to Him. Whether He allows difficulties to arise in our family, finances, or health, He does so out of love. His ultimate purpose is that we become spiritually mature and effective for His kingdom.

We Resist Brokenness because of pride, ignorance, **fear, w**orldly entanglements, unhealthy relationships, **re**belliousness and strongholds of Satan.

Consequences of Resisting Brokenness

A. We hinder our relationship with the Lord.

B. We delay the fulfillment of God's will in our lives.

C. We hurt those who are closest to us.

D. We limit what the Father can do through our gifts and talents.

E. We are "put on the shelf"—unused by the Lord and prevented from experiencing His blessings and future rewards.

What does God keep targeting in your life? Is it your self-reliance? If so, submit to the process of brokenness, and allow Him to control every area of your life. Let Him determine what remains and what must go. Yes, there is suffering in surrendering to the Lord, which may include physical, emotional, spiritual, and even relational pain. But the blessings on the other side of brokenness are most certainly worth it. Our brokenness can affect our finances.

A Personal Checklist To Financial Freedom

Start giving regularly.

Something. Anything. If you don't have money, give your time. Just get the sowing and reaping process started. The Bible says as long as the earth remains there will always be seedtime and harvest and you can't reap what you don't sow. So just like a farmer wouldn't expect crops without planting seed, we too must start sowing in the area that we want to reap.

Make a lifelong promise to yourself to spend less money than you earn.

We could end this checklist right here and it would suffice. Just about everything listed below falls into this category. Spending less than you earn is the key to wealth building, and is the most important lesson when it comes to personal finance. You can do everything else right, but if you spend more money than

you earn. You will not be in a good financial position.

This is the simple rule that allows families living on a $40,000/year salary to retire with millions and that causes millionaires to go bankrupt. You have to decide that you will not spend more money than you earn.

Pay off all consumer debts

Proverbs 22:7 says that the borrower is slave to the lender. Having been a slave and a free man in this area, I much prefer being free. A wonderful second benefit is that you have a lot more financial peace and can build wealth faster when you are out of debt.

Negotiate a better rate with credit card companies

While I was working to pay down my debt, I spent some time on the phone negotiating with my credit card companies to get a better interest rate. It isn't a guarantee, but I consistently would get off the phone with a better interest rate than when I called.

Create a budget

Creating a budget can be as simple or as difficult as you make it. I love having a budget in place contrary to what I thought before I tried it, it doesn't feel like we are in handcuffs, but rather that we are more free to spend money in the areas we want to.

There are lots of budgeting software options and other budgeting tools to help you. Having a budget has helped my marriage, saved us thousands of dollars, and given us so much more peace with our money.

Get the employer match on your 401k

If your employer has a matching program in your 401k or 403b (many of them do) you should try to take advantage of that if at all possible. My former employer had a 100% matching program. So if I put in $500, they put in $500. That is a 100% return on my investment. This is the easiest way to boost your retirement dollars.

Start an emergency fund

This was another thing that we did to give us a lot more peace with our finances. It can be expected that unexpected things will happen. Creating an emergency fund is just proof that you are expecting them.

We have since used our emergency fund to save us even more money.

Sell your junk

Way too many of us have way too much stuff. A lot of it would never be missed if we got rid of it. I have sold a lot of stuff on Ebay & Amazon and it helped provide some extra cash to pay down my debt.

Start learning what the Bible says about Money

The Bible really has a lot to say about our money.

Create a balance sheet

A balance sheet is a snapshot of your financial position. I like to update it every 6 months and it is a fun and helpful way to gauge your progress.

Start giving 10%

Giving 10% of your income to your local church is an important milestone. God was the original giver and we were created by Him to be givers as well. I have witnessed miracles in our life in the area of giving and it also happens to be the only place in the Bible where God says it is okay to test him – See Malachi 3:10.

Organize your bank accounts

I have discovered that having more than one checking account has allowed me to manage my money much cleaner and with more efficiency. Here is a little on how we organize our bank accounts.

Cut Your Expenses

If you are really trying to save money or get out of debt, you need to thoroughly examine each of your monthly expenses. Ask yourself, "Is _____ really necessary?" or "Can I get _____ cheaper somewhere?"

Simplify your bill paying process

I created a simple system for paying my bills each month. It made my life a lot easier and eliminated a lot of stress.

Figure out your true hourly wage

This is a fantastic exercise to help you more accurately know what your time is worth and whether or not that job you have is worth it.

Set Career Goals

Following up on the previous task, is the current job worth it? It is going to help you reach your career goals? If you continue doing what you are doing, where will you be in 5 years – or 20 years? Are you doing what you love? If not, find someone doing what you want to do, take them out to lunch, and ask them how they did it.

Create A Will

Save your loved ones a headache and just do it. You can do it at LegalZoom.com in less than 30 minutes for $69 and be done with it.

Evaluate your car situation

I am convinced that the one of the biggest things that keeps the middle class Americans in the middle class is their insistence on spending way too much of their income on cars. I used to believe that I would always have a car payment. I was wrong and now I intend to never have a car payment because I will save up cash for whatever car I buy.

Start saving for Kid's college

If you have kids you might want to start saving for their college education. Personally, I wouldn't do this until I had my debt paid off and had a head start on saving for retirement. Your kids can take a loan out for college, but the only loan you can get for retirement is on a credit card and that seems a bit foolish to me. Don't you think?

Get Life Insurance

I believe in buying Term Insurance over whole life. There are some cases where there could be an argument for choosing whole life, but generally Term seems to be a better purchase for most people. I recently signed up for my first life insurance policy.

Pay off your house early

As part of getting out of debt, I want to live without a mortgage as well. Just imagine your electric bill being the most expensive bill each month. I can't wait!

Give more than 10%

The more I understand stewardship , the more I realize that every dollar that is in my bank account isn't mine – it is all God's. A big part of being a good steward is understanding this and never letting money get a hold on us. I am convinced that the most fulfilled people in the world are those who always looking for ways to give of themselves. Time, energy, or money – it is in our DNA to be givers and like the parable of the talents teaches us, if we are faithful with small amounts we will be entrusted with more.

CHAPTER 4

Starting Your Own Business

If you're thinking about starting a small business, you should start by weighing the pros and cons, so that you can make a wise decision. The resources in this section are essentially a toolkit to guide your decision-making process.

Consider whether you have the following characteristics and skills commonly associated with successful entrepreneurs:

- **Comfortable with taking risks:** Being your own boss also means you're the one making tough decisions. Entrepreneurship involves uncertainty. Do you avoid uncertainty in life at all costs? If yes, then entrepreneurship may not be the best fit for you. Do you enjoy the thrill of taking calculated risks? Then read on.

- **Independent:** Entrepreneurs have to make a lot of decisions on their own. If you find you can trust your instincts and you're not afraid of rejection every now and then you could be on your way to being an entrepreneur.

- **Persuasive:** You may have the greatest idea in the world, but if you cannot persuade customers, employees and potential lenders or partners, you may find entrepreneurship to be challenging. If you enjoy public speaking, engage new people with ease and find you make compelling arguments grounded in facts, it's likely you're poised to make your idea succeed.

- **Able to negotiate:** As a small business owner, you will need to negotiate everything from leases to contract terms to rates. Polished negotiation skills will help you save money and keep your business running smoothly.

- **Creative:** Are you able to think of new ideas? Can you imagine new ways to solve problems?

- Entrepreneurs must be able to think creatively. If you have insights on how to take advantage of new opportunities, entrepreneurship may be a good fit.

- **Supported by others:** Before you start a business, it's important to have a strong support system in place. You'll be forced to make many important decisions, especially in the first months of opening your business. If you do not have a support network of people to help you, consider finding a business mentor. A business mentor is someone who is experienced, successful and willing to provide advice and guidance.

How to Write a Business Plan

A business plan is an essential roadmap for business success. This living, breathing document generally projects 3-5 years ahead and outlines the route a company intends to take to reach, maintain and grow revenues. A well thought out plan also helps you to step-back and think objectively about the key elements of your business venture and informs your decision-making.

The executive summary is often considered the most important section of a business plan. This section briefly tells your reader where your company is, where you want to take it, and why your business idea will be successful. If you are seeking financing, the executive summary is also your first opportunity to grab a potential investor's interest.

The executive summary should highlight the strengths of your overall plan and therefore be the last section you write. However, it usually appears first in your business plan document.

What to Include in Your Executive Summary

Below are several key points that your executive summary should include based on the stage of your business.

If You Are an Established Business

If you are an established business, be sure to include the following information:

- **The Mission Statement** – This explains what your business is all about. It should be between several sentences and a paragraph.

- **Company Information** – Include a short statement that covers when your business was formed, the names of the founders and their roles, your number of employees, and your business location(s).

- **Growth Highlights** – Include examples of company growth, such as financial or market highlights (for example, "XYZ Firm increased profit margins and market share year-over-year since its foundation). Graphs and charts can be helpful in this section.

- **Your Products/Services** – Briefly describe the products or services you provide.

- **Financial Information** – If you are seeking financing, include any information about your current bank and investors.

- **Summarize future plans** – Explain where you would like to take your business.

With the exception of the mission statement, all of the information in the executive summary should be covered in a concise fashion and kept to one page. The executive summary is the first part of your business plan many people will see, so each word should count.

If You Are a Startup or New Business

If you are just starting a business, you won't have as much information as an established company. Instead, focus on your experience and background as well as the decisions that led you to start this particular enterprise.

Demonstrate that you have done thorough market analysis. Include information about a need or gap in your target market, and how your particular solutions can fill it. Convince the reader that you can succeed in your target market, then address your future plans.

Remember, your Executive Summary will be the last thing you write. So the first section of the business plan that you will tackle is the <u>Market Analysis</u> section.

Market Analysis

The market analysis section of your business plan should illustrate your industry and market knowledge as well as any of your research findings and conclusions. This section is usually presented after the <u>executive summary</u> and the table of contents.

What to Include in Your Market Analysis

Industry Description and Outlook – Describe your industry, including its current size and historic growth rate as well as other trends and characteristics (e.g., life cycle stage, projected growth rate). Next, list the major customer groups within your industry.

Information About Your Target Market – Narrow your target market to a manageable size. Many businesses make the mistake of trying to appeal to too many target markets. Research and include the following information about your market:

Distinguishing characteristics – What are the critical needs of your potential customers? Are those needs being met? What are the demographics of the group and where are they located? Are there any seasonal or cyclical purchasing trends that may impact your business?

Size of the primary target market – In addition to the size of your market, what data can you include about the annual purchases your market makes in your industry? What is the forecasted market growth for this group?.

How much market share can you gain? – What is the market share percentage and number of customers you expect to obtain in a defined geographic area? Explain the logic behind your calculation.

Pricing and gross margin targets – Define your pricing structure, gross margin levels, and any discount that you plan to use.

When you include information about any of the market tests or research studies you have completed, be sure to focus only on the results of these tests. Any other details should be included in the appendix.

Competitive Analysis – Your competitive analysis should identify your competition by product line or service and market segment. Assess the following characteristics of the competitive landscape:

- Market share
- Strengths and weaknesses
- How important is your target market to your competitors?
- Are there any barriers that may hinder you as you enter the market?

- What is your window of opportunity to enter the market?
- Are there any indirect or secondary competitors who may impact your success?
- What barriers to market are there (e.g., changing technology, high investment cost, lack of quality personnel)?

Regulatory Restrictions – Include any customer or governmental regulatory requirements affecting your business, and how you'll comply. Also, cite any operational or cost impact the compliance process will have on your business.

Once you've completed this section you can move on to the Company Description section of your business plan.

Funding

- Are your needs short-term or long-term? How quickly will you be able to pay back the loan or provide return on their investment?
- Is the money for operating expenses or for capital expenditures that will become assets, such as equipment or real estate?
- Do you need all the money now or in smaller pieces over several months?
- Are you willing to assume all the risk if your company doesn't succeed, or do you want someone to share the risk?

Fundamentally, there are two types of business financing:

- **Debt financing** - You borrow the money and agree to pay it back in a particular time frame at a set interest rate. You owe the money whether your venture succeeds or not. Bank loans are what most people typically think of as debt financing, but we will explore many other options below.

- **Equity financing** - You sell partial ownership of your company in exchange for cash. The investors assume all (or most) of the risk--if the company fails, they lose their money. But if it succeeds, they typically make *much* greater return on their investment than interest rates. In other words, equity financing is far more expensive if your company is successful, but far less expensive if it isn't.

Because investors take on a much higher risk than lenders, they are typically far more involved in your company. This can be a mixed blessing. They will likely offer advice and connections to help grow your business. But if their plan is to exit your company in 2-3 years with a substantial return on their investment, and your motivation is the long-term sustainable growth of the company, you may find yourself at odds with them as the company grows. Be careful not to give up too much control of your company.

Let's take a closer look at the many options available for startups.

Friends and family are still your best source for both loans and equity deals. They are typically less stringent regarding your credit and their expected return on investment. One caveat: structure the deal with the same legal rigor you would with anyone else or it may create problems down the road when you look for additional financing. Prepare a business plan and formal documents--you'll both feel better, and it's good practice for later.

Credit cards are a great tool for cash flow management, assuming you use them just for that and not for long-term financing. Keep one or two cards with no balance on it and pay it off every month to give yourself a 30 to 60 day float with no interest. And the low introductory rates on some cards make them some of the cheapest money around. Managed well, they're extremely effective; managed poorly, they're extremely expensive.

Bank loans come in all shapes and sizes, from microloans of a few hundred dollars, typically offered by local community banks, to six-figure loans by major national banks. These are much easier to obtain when backed by assets (home equity or an IRA) or third-party guarantors (e.g., government-sponsored SBA loans or a cosigner). If you obtain a line of credit rather than a fixed-amount loan, you don't start paying interest until you actually spend the money.

Leasing is the way to go if you need big-ticket items such as equipment, vehicles, or even computers. Your supplier will help you explore this.

Angel investors fill the gap between friends and family and venture capitalists, who now rarely even look at investments below $1 million. Enlist a savvy financial adviser to structure the deal.

Private lending represents a viable alternative when the bank says "no". Private lenders are looking for the same information and will conduct similar due diligence as the banks, but they typically specialize in an industry and are more willing to take on higher-risk loans if they see the potential.

There are many channels available to you to raise capital. All of the above approaches have numerous variations. Put together a solid business plan, talk to a financial adviser, and just start asking. Someone will eventually say "Yes".

Preparation: The Key to Small Business Loans

In order to prove that you're worth the money, you'll want to prepare some documentation. First, your personal credit history is relevant to your small business loan especially if your business does not have a long operating history. They will assume that you operate your business in the same manner that you manage your personal finances. Bring your credit history with you to reference as necessary.

Next, bring financial statements for your business. You'll need to show your business's financial health. They want to know how much it's worth and how much money you're moving. If you're serious about small business loans, then you'll also want to prepare detailed pro-forma statements. These give projections about what your business will be worth going forward.

Finally, be sure you have an updated business plan. By preparing a detailed business plan, you'll already have your financial statements and pro-formas prepared. Banks award small business loans to those that have everything spelled out and planned. I strongly suggest that you prepare a plan with as much detail as possible – including bios of you and your partners, your track record, your strategies and advantages, and more.

Choosing Banks for Small Business Loans

After you've prepared your documentation, it's time to walk in and ask for the money. Where should you go for your small business loan? Since you'll have to share ALL of your personal and business

financial information anyway, do it with somebody who already has that information.

Start with institutions that you already do business with. These places know your history and financial behavior, and they're more likely to give small business loans to those who've demonstrated financial responsibility. Remember, a big part of the bank's risk is uncertainty regarding loan repayment. If they can reduce uncertainty about you, you're in a better position. If you have your mortgage with a bank, that's a good place to start asking about small business loans.

If you can't or won't use your existing relationships, go to somebody who *wants* the business. Search the business section of your newspaper for financing offers. These banks are actively looking for small business loans and the process may be easier with them.

Another choice is to ask around at credit unions. Because these institutions are smaller, you may be able to talk directly with higher-level decision makers to plead your case. Larger banks have more rigid rules and processes associated with small business loans. Even if the person you're talking to believes in you, he or she may not be able to help.

Do You Need an EIN?

You will need an EIN.

WARNING - Be aware of suspected phishing scheme in <u>email claiming to be from IRS' Office of Professional Responsibility.</u>

Daily Limitation of an Employer Identification Number

Effective May 21, 2012, to ensure fair and equitable treatment for all taxpayers, the Internal Revenue Service will limit Employer Identification Number (EIN) issuance to one per <u>responsible party</u> per day. This limitation is applicable to all requests for EINs whether online or by phone, fax or mail. We apologize for any inconvenience this may cause.

Do you have employees?	<u>YES</u>	NO

Do you operate your business as a corporation or a partnership?	YES	NO
Do you file any of these tax returns: Employment, Excise, or Alcohol, Tobacco and Firearms?	YES	NO
Do you withhold taxes on income, other than wages, paid to a non-resident alien?	YES	NO
Do you have a Keogh plan?	YES	NO
Are you involved with any of the following types of organizations? • Trusts, except certain grantor-owned revocable trusts, IRAs, Exempt Organization Business Income Tax Returns • Estates • Real estate mortgage investment conduits • Non-profit organizations • Farmers' cooperatives • Plan administrators	YES	NO

Deducting Business Expenses

Business expenses are the cost of carrying on a trade or business. These expenses are usually deductible if the business is operated to make a profit.

What Can I Deduct?

To be deductible, a business expense must be both ordinary and necessary. An ordinary expense is one that is common and accepted in your trade or business. A necessary expense is one that is helpful and appropriate for your trade or business. An expense does not have to be indispensable to be considered necessary.

It is important to separate business expenses from the following expenses:

• The expenses used to figure the cost of goods sold,

• Capital Expenses, and

• Personal Expenses.

Cost of Goods Sold

If your business manufactures products or purchases them for resale, you generally must value inventory at the beginning and end of each tax year to determine your cost of goods sold. Some of your expenses may be included in figuring the cost of goods sold. Cost of goods sold is deducted from your gross receipts to figure your gross profit for the year. If you include an expense in the cost of goods sold, you cannot deduct it again as a business expense.

The following are types of expenses that go into figuring the cost of goods sold.

- The cost of products or raw materials, including freight
- Storage
- Direct labor costs (including contributions to pensions or annuity plans) for workers who produce the products
- Factory overhead

Under the uniform capitalization rules, you must capitalize the direct costs and part of the indirect costs for certain production or resale activities. Indirect costs include rent, interest, taxes, storage, purchasing, processing, repackaging, handling, and administrative costs.

This rule does not apply to personal property you acquire for resale if your average annual gross receipts (or those of your predecessor) for the preceding 3 tax years are not more than $10 million.

For additional information, refer to Publication 334, Tax Guide for Small Businesses and the chapter on Inventories, Publication 538, Accounting Periods and Methods.

Capital Expenses

You must capitalize, rather than deduct, some costs. These costs are a part of your investment in your business and are called capital expenses. Capital expenses are considered assets in your business. There are, in general, three types of costs you capitalize.

- Business start-up cost

- Business assets
- Improvements

Personal versus Business Expenses

Generally, you cannot deduct personal, living, or family expenses. However, if you have an expense for something that is used partly for business and partly for personal purposes, divide the total cost between the business and personal parts. You can deduct the business part.

For example, if you borrow money and use 70% of it for business and the other 30% for a family vacation, you can deduct 70% of the interest as a business expense. The remaining 30% is personal interest and is not deductible.

Business Use of Your Home

If you use part of your home for business, you may be able to deduct expenses for the business use of your home. These expenses may include mortgage interest, insurance, utilities, repairs, and depreciation.

Business Use of Your Car

If you use your car in your business, you can deduct car expenses. If you use your car for both business and personal purposes, you must divide your expenses based on actual mileage.

Other Types of Business Expenses

- **Employees' Pay** - You can generally deduct the pay you give your employees for the services they perform for your business.
- **Retirement Plans** - Retirement plans are savings plans that offer you tax advantages to set aside money for your own, and your employees' retirement.
- **Rent Expense** - Rent is any amount you pay for the use of property you do not own. In general, you can deduct rent as an expense only if the rent is for property you use in your trade or business. If you have or will receive equity in or title to the property, the rent is not deductible.

- **Interest** - Business interest expense is an amount charged for the use of money you borrowed for business activities.
- **Taxes** - You can deduct various federal, state, local, and foreign taxes directly attributable to your trade or business as business expenses.
- **Insurance** - Generally, you can deduct the ordinary and necessary cost of insurance as a business expense, if it is for your trade, business, or profession.

Income Tax

All businesses except partnerships must file an annual income tax return. Partnerships file an information return. The form you use depends on how your business is organized. The federal income tax is a pay-as-you-go tax. You must pay the tax as you earn or receive income during the year. An employee usually has income tax withheld from his or her pay. If you do not pay your tax through withholding, or do not pay enough tax that way, you might have to pay estimated tax. If you are not required to make estimated tax payments, you may pay any tax due when you file your return.

Estimated tax

Generally, you must pay taxes on income, including self-employment tax (discussed next), by making regular payments of estimated tax during the year.

Self-Employment Tax

Self-employment tax (SE tax) is a social security and Medicare tax primarily for individuals who work for themselves. Your payments of SE tax contribute to your coverage under the social security system. Social security coverage provides you with retirement benefits, disability benefits, survivor benefits, and hospital insurance (Medicare) benefits.

Generally, you must pay SE tax and file Schedule SE (Form 1040) if either of the following applies.

- If your net earnings from self-employment were $400 or more.
- If you work for a church or a qualified church-controlled organization (other than as a minister or

member of a religious order) that elected an exemption from social security and Medicare taxes, you are subject to SE tax if you receive $108.28 or more in wages from the church or organization.

Note: There are Special Rules and Exceptions for aliens, fishing crew members, notary public, State or local government employees, foreign government or international organization employees, etc.

Employment Taxes

When you have employees, you as the employer have certain employment tax responsibilities that you must pay and forms you must file. Employment taxes include the following:

- Social security and Medicare taxes
- Federal income tax withholding
- Federal unemployment (FUTA) tax

Excise Tax

This section describes the excise taxes you may have to pay and the forms you have to file if you do any of the following.

- Manufacture or sell certain products.
- Operate certain kinds of businesses.
- Use various kinds of equipment, facilities, or products.
- Receive payment for certain services.

Form 720 - The federal excise taxes reported on <u>Form 720</u> (PDF), consist of several broad categories of taxes, including the following.

- Environmental taxes.
- Communications and air transportation taxes.
- Fuel taxes.
- Tax on the first retail sale of heavy trucks, trailers, and tractors.

- Manufacturers taxes on the sale or use of a variety of different articles

Form 2290 - There is a federal excise tax on certain trucks, truck tractors, and buses used on public

highways. The tax applies to vehicles having a taxable gross weight of 55,000 pounds or more. **Form 730** - If you are in the business of accepting wagers or conducting a wagering pool or lottery, you may be liable for the federal excise tax on wagering

Form 11-C - Use Form 11-C, Occupational Tax and Registration Return for Wagering, to register for any wagering activity and to pay the federal occupational tax on wagering.

Excise Tax has several general excise tax programs. One of the major components of the excise program is motor fuel.

Evaluate and Develop Your Business Idea

Step	Description
1	Determine if the type of business suits you.
2	Use a break-even analysis to determine if your idea can make money.
3	Write a business plan, including a profit/loss forecast and a cash flow analysis.
4	Find sources of start-up financing.
5	Set up a basic marketing plan.

Decide on a Legal Structure for Your Business

6	Identify the number of owners of your business.
7	Decide how much protection from personal liability you'll need, which depends on your business's risks.
8	Decide how you'd like the business to be taxed.

9   Consider whether your business would benefit from being able to sell stock.

10. Research the various types of ownership structures.

11   Get more in-depth information from a self-help resource before you settle on a structure. If you are unsure, talk to a lawyer.

Choose a Name for Your Business

12   Think of several business names that might suit your company and its products or services.

13   If you will do business online, check if your proposed business names are available as domain names.

14   Check with your county clerk's office to see whether your proposed names are on the list of fictitious or assumed business names in your county.

15   For corporations and LLCs: check the availability of your proposed names with the Secretary of State or other corporate filing office.

16   Do a federal or state trademark search of the proposed names still on your list. If a proposed name is being used as a trademark, eliminate it if your use of the name would confuse customers or if the name is already famous.

17   Choose between the proposed names that are still on your list.

Register Your Business Name

18   Register your business name with your county clerk as a fictitious or assumed business name, if necessary.

19   Register your business name as a federal or state trademark if you'll do

business regionally or nationally and will use your business name to identify a product or service.

20   Register your business name as a domain name if you'll use the name as a Web address too.

Prepare Organizational Paperwork

21   Partnership

22   LLC

23   C Corporation

24   S Corporation

Things You Should Know Before Starting a Business

The main reason for starting a business varies from person to person. Before moving ahead you should honestly evaluate yourself. Identify your positives and negatives. All people are not made to become entrepreneurs. There are serious risks involved in business. It can drastically change your lifestyle.

What are the things you should consider before starting your own business?

1. Desire to Succeed

Most people jump into business, when they get a brilliant idea. But this initial enthusiasm wanes when they face disappointments. You should have a great desire to succeed. There should be constant motivating factors.

2. Identify Your Niche

Once you have decided to start a business, you need to identify your niche. The choices are unlimited. But your business idea should strike a balance with your financial reserve. You should also decide on the community you intend to serve. When starting a business, look for a niche where there is not much competition. Competing with well-established players in the initial stage of your business will do more harm than good.

3. Innovation

Finding a market without competitors is not easy. In fact, there is competition in every sector. But all markets can accommodate new players. The survival of the new entrants depends upon their innovativeness. Before starting a business, you need to do your homework. You need to study the market in detail. Find out new service areas or target those areas that are not properly served. Create an innovative business concept.

4. Extensive Research

You have a great idea. But, what if people do not want your product or service? The idea is great for you but not for the customers. So, before starting a business, you need make sure that your product or service has potential buyers. Find out the results of similar ideas in other markets. Do an extensive research to make sure that your idea will work out as planned.

5. Financial Matter

Once you have decided on a product or service for business, you need to look into the financial matters. Money comes into play from the day you decided to start a business. Even the initial research needs money. Some business needs huge investment and some as little as few hundred dollars. Before starting a business, make a rough estimate of the money needed. Identify the sources from which you are going to raise the needed money. Make sure that these sources will serve you throughout the initial phase. Most business run into trouble mainly due to the lack of funds.

6. Savings

If you have relinquished your job to start the business, you should have enough saving to sustain you for at least two years. Having a part time job will be of great help during the initial years of your business. This will provide the much needed flexibility in financial matters.

7. Identify Your Business Role

You need to clearly identify your role in the business. This is not a problem, if your business is a one-man show. But if you need to divide the responsibilities, you need to be very careful. Make sure that the employees understand your idea and vision. Even after dividing the responsibilities, you should scrutinize the activities periodically. The appointment of employees also involves several legal nuances. In the initial phase, you should keep your business simple with fewer employees and less investment.

8. Legal Matters

The legal matters are not confined to the appointment of employees. Even before starting a business, you should take the advice of a legal professional. A lawyer will be able to point out the legal difficulties involved in your business idea. To run a business, you need to observe several laws. As a novice to business, you might not understand the right spirit of these laws. In such a situation, it is wise to take the advice of a lawyer. A lawyer will be able to protect your business by creating contracts and other documents.

9. Checklist of Essentials

Before starting a business, make a checklist of all the essentials needed. Take each item in the checklist and analyze it. This will give a better control over the matters. Prepare realistic goals. And make all effort to achieve it.

CHAPTER 5

Scholarships

A college scholarship is the money available to college students to pursue their education and fulfill their dreams. Scholarships are sponsored by government and non-government organizations and are made available to students who fit a certain profile such as merit, gender, race or program of study. Students are not required to return college scholarship money. A recent survey states that more than $134 Billion are available in scholarships. Therefore, you should not hesitate from searching and applying for a scholarship. As a matter of fact you can attend any college for free if you know how to look for a scholarship.

How to get a College Scholarship

Every student would like to get a scholarship so that they can get their education for free. The good news is that there are plenty of scholarships available. All you need to know is when and how to apply for. Things which can help you get a scholarship:

- Good academic record
- Involvement in Athletics or Sports
- Involvement in Extracurricular activities
- Involvement in Community
- Being a woman
- Being a minority such as Hispanic, African American, Asian, native American, east Indian, Japanese, Korean, Pakistani, Iranian, Russian
- Great writing skills
- Great speaking skills
- Demonstrated Financial Need
- Great Attitude

What kind of College Scholarships are available

If you can think of type, there is probably a scholarship available. We have scholarships for women, minorities, subjects, athletes, Hispanics, African Americans, Asian, Native Americans, east Indians, Christians, Jews, you just name it. All of the scholarships on our site are generous donations by corporations.

Scholarship Search is Free

We offer free scholarship listing. This site is absolutely free and does not cost you even a single penny. All you need is a good internet connection. You can even browse our scholarships using Apple's iPhone, iPod, Google's Android, Microsoft's Windows Phone and Nokia's Android Phones.

Aggregated by a Successful Financial Aid and Scholarship Recipient

The founder of this site is a successful immigrant, who has received his bachelor's degree in engineering and an MBA both by taking financial aid, grants, scholarships and student loans. Now he feels that it is his turn to give back to the community by hosting this free site. He also feels that scholarship listing should be unbiased and available to users on their fingertips.

Largest Scholarships for High School Senior

Name	Amount	Deadline
Voice of Democracy Scholarship Competition	$30000	November 01, 2012
American Legion National High School Oratorical Contest	$18000	Varies
National Merit Semi-Finalist Scholarship - CIU	$11750	Varies
Coca-Cola Scholars Program	$20000	October 31, 2012
Junior Achievement Essay Competition - National Capital Area	$20000	October 31, 2012
Susan G. Komen for the Cure College Scholarship	$10000	October 15, 2012
Ventures Scholars Program	$10000	Varies
Eagle Scout of the Year Scholarship	$10000	March 01, 2013
Major Don S. Gentile Scholarship	$6000	Varies
Alphonse A. Miele Scholarship	$6000	Varies

New Scholarships for High School Senior

Name	Amount	Deadline
Bill and Jane Kerbey Scholarship	Varies	Varies
Trevett, Cristo, Salzer and Andolina Dual Credit Scholarship	Varies	Varies
Balanced Man Scholarship - University of Nebraska, Omaha	$1000	Varies
Jenkins Family Scholarship	Varies	Varies
Baron Family Scholarship	Varies	Varies
Balanced Man Scholarship - Georgia Alpha	$500	Varies
Balanced Man Scholarship - University of Nevada, Reno	Varies	Varies
Balanced Man Scholarship - University of Oregon	$1000	Varies
Balanced Man Scholarship - University of Tennessee, Martin	$1500	Varies
ProStart Scholarship - Johnson Wales University	Varies	Varies

Largest Scholarships for High School Juniors

Name	Amount	Deadline
Voice of Democracy Scholarship Competition	$30000	November 01, 2012
American Legion National High School Oratorical Contest	$18000	Varies
Eagle Scout of the Year Scholarship	$10000	March 01, 2013
Junior Achievement Essay Competition - National Capital Area	$20000	October 31, 2012
Ventures Scholars Program	$10000	Varies
First Freedom Student Competition	$2500	November 26, 2012
CaptainU $2000 Student-Athlete Scholarship	$2000	September 30, 2012
College Prowler $2,000 No Essay Scholarship	$2000	September 30, 2012
Cedar Valley Science Symposium Scholarship	$1500	Varies
Siemens Competition	$100000	October 01, 2012

Apply for Scholarships

The only way to have a shot at <u>winning scholarships</u> is to apply for scholarships. You'll hear it from us time and time again apply early, and apply often. If you miss a deadline and send your application in late, you go to the bottom of the pile. If you skip out on an award because you think you don't have a good shot at landing that award, you could be missing out on an opportunity for some generous funding, and free funding that you won't need to pay back. The more <u>scholarship information</u> you have, the more prepared you'll be to start the process and land your share of the free money out there to supplement your financial aid package for college. Even better, take a few minutes to <u>conduct a free, college scholarship search</u> to find scholarships for which you may be eligible.

The Scholarship Search

You may feel like scholarship awards are too competitive for you to be eligible for many, but someone has to win, so why shouldn't it be you? There are ways to improve your chances at landing a scholarship, even if it's the most competitive scholarship with the biggest reward. Target academic scholarships if you have a stellar GPA and standardized test scores, but also make a list of what makes you unique and make sure to include those characteristics when you're filling out your profile or looking to outside sources for potential scholarship sources.

Once you've got a good list going of scholarships you're eligible for, it's time to go over those results and make the ones with approaching deadlines and those you feel you have the best shot at winning your top priority. (If you don't match the criteria of an award, don't apply. There are too many scholarships out there that will fit your unique student characteristics that you shouldn't be wasting your time on awards you don't fit the eligibility requirements for.) Don't be shy about contacting scholarship providers and declaring your candidacy for this year's winner. Be sure you contact each provider in the manner they've requested, whether its email, fax or formal letter, as it's important that you follow the directions of any scholarship application to the letter. To maximize your scholarship application output and the scholarships you'll receive, be sure to start as early as possible, usually in October of your senior year of high school. Also, be sure to keep your profile up-to-date so you can find out about new opportunities and send them a scholarship application.

The Application Process

When you're ready to start applying, it's important to get organized. One of the most important steps once you find an award that interests you is to read the directions, qualifications, and fine print carefully (an award you have to pay for to receive could be a scholarship scam). You may even find some of the work you do can be applied to multiple scholarship applications such as an essay or writing sample. (Be sure you read the directions for those essays carefully, though. Make sure you're answering the essay question accurately and thoughtfully, as many judges will look to those essays to narrow down a long list of applicants.) Start working on those essays early, and ask teachers or your peers for honest feedback.   If it sounds too easy, that's because it actually is easy to apply for scholarships. Some may require that you to put in some time, but once you've completed an application or two you might find it will get easier and take less time with each additional one. Don't psych yourself out or let yourself get overwhelmed by all you need to do before you graduate high school. Start early and work diligently and it will pay off. And remember: you're not alone. Many students feel unprepared when they're starting the process, but will a little research, preparation and help from Scholarships.com, you could be on your way to an impressive financial aid package.

Tips for Formatting Scholarship Application Essays

When you are preparing a scholarship application essay, make sure to pay as much attention to the scholarship essay format as you do to the content. Individuals who judge college scholarship essay contests look very closely at the essays they receive and evaluate them based on content, writing style, adherence to instructions and format. The first thing they notice is the format. As you know, you never get a second chance to make a first impression so be sure the format of your essay is both professional and visually appealing.

Scholarship Essay Formatting Tips:

- The most important tip is to be certain that you follow all formatting instructions specified for the scholarship contest.

- Print your essay on high quality paper. Most applicants will use standard copy paper and your essay will stand out if it is on a better type of paper.

- Use a font that is professional in appearance and easy to read. Recommended fonts include: Arial, Calibri, Tahoma, Times New Roman and Verdana. Do not use a script or "cute" style font.

- Do not use a font that is too small or too large. If a font size is not specified in the instructions, use a size between 10 and 12 points for the body of your essay and 14 points for the heading.

- If your printer is running low on ink, replace the toner or ink jet before printing your final copy.

- Make sure there are no smudges or unnecessary creases on the paper.

- Do not fold the essay or application form. Use an envelope large enough to hold all documents without folding them unless the instructions specify a smaller envelope.

- Make sure your essay is free of typos, grammatical errors and spelling mistakes.

- Even if you have proofread your essay several times, get someone else to proofread it before you send it in.

Delaware State University

Inspire Scholarship

Requirements

The Basics:

- Be regularly admitted and enroll in the fall semester immediately following graduation from a Delaware public or non-public high school

- Earn a minimum cumulative GPA of 2.75 or higher on a 4.0 scale, as indicated on the student's official high school transcript

- Complete the FAFSA by March 15 and accept all forms of financial aid for which the student is eligible, except for loans

- Have no felony convictions

- Complete 10 hours of community service, as defined by the institution, each semester at DSU

The Details:

The Inspire Scholarship is available to Delaware high school graduates with excellent credentials to attend Delaware State University. The intent of this program is to offset the cost of tuition, thereby increasing the number of Delawareans who attend college and complete degree programs. The scholarship program is subject to available funds appropriated by the Delaware General Assembly. Inspire scholarship recipients must continue to make excellent academic progress toward a degree and must complete at least ten hours of community service per semester.

1. A student must be admitted and attend classes at Delaware State University no later than the fall semester immediately after the student's graduation from a Delaware public or non-public high school.

   To be eligible for the Inspire Scholarship program, a student must satisfy Delaware residency requirements as set forth in Delaware State University's residency policy and be enrolled full-time on a degree-seeking basis. Students with a disability must comply with Delaware State University's academic accommodation policy.

   A student must graduate from a Delaware public or non-public high school with a minimum cumulative grade point average (GPA) of 2.75 or higher on a 4.0 scale as indicated on the student's official high school transcript. Home-schooled students will abide by the same standards as public and non-public Delaware high school graduates.

2. The student must not have been convicted of any felony, and the student and parent/legal guardian or relative caregiver must certify such fact. If a student has felony charges pending, the student and parent/legal guardian or relative caregiver will sign a certification that if the student is convicted of a felony, the student, parent/legal guardian or relative caregiver will notify the Office of Financial Aid at Delaware State University, and the student will no longer be eligible for the Inspire Scholarship.

3. A student must satisfy admission standards as determined by Delaware State University and must be enrolled in a degree-seeking program.

4. A student must complete 10 hours of community service, as defined by the institution, per semester.

5. A student must submit the Free Application for Federal Student Aid (FAFSA The DSU school code is 001428**),** and accept all appropriate forms of financial aid for which the student is eligible including, but not limited to, the Federal Pell Grant, financial aid programs administered by the Delaware Higher Education Commission, and financial aid programs administered by Delaware State University, except for loans. If other forms of financial aid (not including loans) cover full tuition, the Inspire Scholarship will NOT be awarded. If financial aid funds do NOT cover full tuition, the Inspire Scholarship will be awarded to cover the difference up to the maximum of $3,000 per year.

A student should apply for financial aid by the priority deadline date of March 15 of each year. Students meeting the March 15 priority deadline will be given first priority for the Inspire Scholarship in the event the number of eligible scholarship recipients exceeds funding appropriated by the Delaware General Assembly.

6. A final official academic transcript must be received by the Office of Admissions at Delaware State University no later than June 30 of each year to verify graduation and final cumulative GPA.

How to Apply

To apply, follow these steps*

1. **Apply for financial aid by submitting a Free Application for Federal Student Aid (FAFSA)** by the priority deadline of **March 15** to the federal processor
2. (FAFSA available after January 1). The DSU school code is 001428.
3. Submit a complete **Application for Admission** with a one-time, non-refundable $35 application fee to attend the fall semester. Paper applications may be requested by phone, mail, via the Web (www.desu.edu/admissions), or from your high school counselor. Apply early for admission!
4. Provide official scores from the SAT/ACT tests to the Office of Admissions at Delaware State University.
5. Submit your final official high school transcript by June 30 to the Office of Admissions.

6. Upon completion of the above requirements, the Office of Financial Aid will notify you of your Inspire eligibility.

* The Inspire Scholarship will be subject to available appropriations for each fiscal year.

(Top)

How to Maintain Eligibility

Listed below are the requirements to maintain eligibility in the Inspire Scholarship program.

1. A student must complete 12 or more eligible credits in both fall and spring semesters. The student must make steady satisfactory academic progress toward a degree, earning no fewer than 24 credit hours required for full-time status in each academic year.
2. A student must maintain continuous full-time enrollment for both the fall and spring semesters in each successive academic year, unless granted an exception for cause by the University Scholarship Council.
3. A student must maintain a cumulative grade point average of at least 2.75 calculated on a 4.0 scale. Cumulative grade point average will be verified the day after summer session grades are reviewed to determine eligibility for the upcoming academic year.
4. The student and parent/legal guardian or relative caregiver will notify the Office of Financial Aid if at any time during the award period there are felony charges pending against the student, and the student and parent/legal guardian or relative caregiver will sign a certification that if the student is convicted of a felony at any time during the award period, the student, parent/legal guardian or relative caregiver will notify the Office of Financial Aid, and the student will no longer be eligible for the Inspire Scholarship.
5. Students are eligible to participate in the Inspire Scholarship program for a period not to exceed six (6) continuous semesters, whether or not Inspire payment is made. Summer sessions are not included in the six semester calculation.
6. The Inspire Scholarship will not pay for courses or other post-secondary units previously paid or taken in excess of the requirement for completion of a bachelor's degree.

7. A student must complete 10 hours of community service, as defined by the institution, per semester.

8. Students are not eligible for Inspire Scholarship payment for summer session classes and will be personally responsible for payment of summer session classes.

9. To maintain eligibility for the Inspire Scholarship during the next academic year, the student should reapply for financial aid by March 15 of each year.

Delaware Technical and Community College Seed Program

Scholarship Requirements

Student Excellent Equals Degree (SEED) Scholarship Requirements

1. You shall be admitted and attend classes at Delaware Technical Community College no later than the fall semester immediately after the student's graduation from a Delaware public or non-public high school.

- To be eligible for the SEED Scholarship program, you must satisfy Delaware residency requirements as set forth in Delaware Tech's residency policy and be enrolled full-time on a degree-seeking basis. If you have a disability, you must comply with Delaware Tech's academic accommodation policy.

- You shall have graduated from a Delaware public or non-public high school with a minimum cumulative average of either 80 or higher on a 100 point scale, a grade point average (GPA) of 2.5 or higher on a 4.0 scale as indicated on the student's official high school transcript, or a letter grade of C+. Since high schools use different methods for reporting grades (letter, number or GPA), the minimum acceptable academic requirement shall be: GPA of 2.5, 80 for numerical and C+ for letter grade.

- The equivalency standards for Delaware home-schooled students shall be a complete home schooled academic transcript, or a combined score of 1350 on the new SAT or a composite ACT score of at least 19.

- If you are an undocumented student, you must meet the same eligibility requirements as documented students regarding attendance immediately from high school, academics (GPA), felony convictions and enrollment as a full-time student. To qualify as an undocumented scholarship recipient, the student must have: (a) attended a high school located within the State of Delaware for two or more years; (b) graduated from a Delaware high school; (c) applied for all campus-based financial aid (scholarships, etc.) for which s/he would be eligible; and (d) submit a notarized Tuition Affidavit (available in Delaware Tech's Financial Aid Office) which certifies that the student is an undocumented person and that s/he has filed an application to legalize his/her immigration status or will file an application to legalize his/her application status as soon as s/he is eligible.

2. You shall not have been convicted of any felony and the student and your parent/legal guardian or relative caregiver shall certify such fact.

- If you have felony charges pending, you and your parent/legal guardian or relative caregiver will need to sign a certification stating that if you are convicted of a felony, you, your parent/legal guardian or relative caregiver will notify the appropriate Delaware Tech Financial Aid Office, and you will no longer be eligible for the SEED Scholarship.

3. You shall have satisfied <u>admission standards</u> as determined by Delaware Tech and must be enrolled in a degree-seeking program.

- This includes applying for all appropriate forms of financial aid by filling out the Free Application for Federal Student Aid (FAFSA), by the priority deadline of April 1 of each year, and accepting all such financial assistance offered or awarded, except for loans. The FAFSA available online at www.fafsa.ed.gov You must complete all institutional forms and supporting documentation as requested by your campus.

- If you receive notice that you are eligible for a Pell Grant and it covers full tuition, the SEED Scholarship will NOT be awarded. If Pell Grant funds do not cover full tuition, the SEED Scholarship WILL be awarded to cover the difference.

4. A student must complete and return the SEED Scholarship application to the appropriate Delaware Tech Financial Aid Office no later than April 15 of each year. A student who applies for the SEED Scholarship after the April 15 priority deadline date will be considered for the SEED Scholarship under the second priority awarding, which will be subject to available funding for each fiscal year.

5. A final official academic transcript must be received by the appropriate Delaware Tech Financial Aid Office no later than June 30 of each year to verify graduation and final cumulative GPA.

6. Current high school graduates meeting all eligibility requirements who did not apply for Year 1 SEED Scholarship may qualify to apply for Year 2 as long as all other requirements related to enrollment and eligibility at Delaware Tech are met.

How to Apply for State Aid

The Delaware Higher Education Office administers 23 state-sponsored financial aid programs and 7 private scholarship programs to help Delawareans continue their education after high school. Unless otherwise noted, applicants for state-funded programs must be Delaware residents and U.S. citizens or eligible noncitizens.

For programs below followed by an asterisk (*), you must complete the **Common Merit Application**. These programs include:

Academic Memorial Scholarships

Academic Scholarships

Professional Incentive Programs (both undergraduate and graduate).

Private Scholarships Administered by the Higher Education Commission in DE.

Delaware Engineering Society Scholarships

Delaware Open Cross Country Championship Scholarship

Delaware Solid Waste Authority John P. "Pat" Healy Scholarship

First State Manufactured Housing Scholarship

Port of Wilmington Maritime Society Scholarship

Joseph B. Schafferman, Sr. Memorial Scholarship Fund

CHAPTER 6

Grants

What is a grant and how does it work?

Grants are not benefits or entitlements. A federal grant is an award of financial assistance from a federal agency to a recipient to carry out a public purpose of support or stimulation authorized by a law of the United States. Federal grants are not federal assistance or loans to individuals.

A federal grant may not be used to acquire property or services for the federal government's direct benefit. The 26 federal agencies offer over 1,000 grant programs annually in various categories.

Grants.gov is your source to FIND and APPLY for federal grants. The U.S. Department of Health and Human Services is proud to be the managing partner for Grants.gov, an initiative that is having an unparalleled impact on the grant community. Learn more about Grants.gov and determine if you are eligible for grant opportunities offered on this site.

Tips on Applying

- Always contact the official listed in the request for application or program announcement with questions about a specific grant.

- Grants.gov Applicant Resources – There are several tools and documents available.

- Obtaining a DUNS number (PDF-15.2KB) – All federal agencies require all applicants to provide a Dun and Bradstreet (D&B) Data Universal Numbering System (DUNS) number when applying for Federal grants or cooperative agreements.

- "Developing Competitive SAMHSA Grant Applications" Participant Manual (browse or download as PDF) – This manual was developed to provide organizations with skills and resources needed to plan and write a competitive SAMHSA grant application. Although written with SAMHSA programs in mind, information in this manual is helpful for individuals applying for any federal grant.

- "Tips for Novice Grant Seekers" – Information compiled by the Center for Faith-based and

Neighborhood Partnerships at the Department of Education

- <u>SAMHSA Grants-Writing Training and Technical Assistance Trainings</u> for Grassroots Faith and Community Based Groups

- <u>The Foundation Center</u> offers a large selection of training for organizations seeking assistance with all steps of the grant seeking process.

Grants.gov does not provide personal financial assistance. To learn where you may find personal help.

GRANT CATEGORIES

More than 1,000 grant programs are offered by the 26 federal grant-making agencies, and these programs fall into 21 categories

Agriculture

Arts

Business and Commerce

Community Development

Disaster Prevention and Relief

Education

Employment, Labor and Training

Energy

Environmental Quality

Food and Nutrition

Health

Housing

Humanities

Information and Statistics

Law, Justice and Legal Services

Natural Resources

Recovery Act

Regional Development

Science and Technology

Social Services and Income Security

Transportation

There are many groups of organizations that are eligible to apply for government grants. Typically, most grantee organizations fall into the categories below.

Government Organizations

- State Governments
- Local Governments
- City or Township Governments
- Special District Governments
- Native American Tribal Governments (federally recognized)
- Native American Tribal Governments (other than federally recognized)

Education Organizations

- Independent School Districts
- Public and State Controlled Institutions of Higher Education
- Private Institutions of Higher Education

Public Housing Organizations

- Public Housing Authorities
- Indian Housing Authorities

Non-Profit Organizations

- Nonprofits having a 501(c)(3) status with the IRS, other than institutions of higher education
- Nonprofits that do not have a 501(c)(3) status with the IRS, other than institutions of higher education

For-Profit Organizations (other than small businesses)

Small Businesses

Small business loans and small business grants may be awarded to companies that meet the size standards that the U.S. Small Business Administration (SBA) has established for most industries in the economy. The most common size standards are as follows:

- 500 employees for most manufacturing and mining industries
- 100 employees for all wholesale trade industries
- $6 million for most retail and service industries
- $28.5 million for most general & heavy construction industries
- $12 million for all special trade contractors
- $0.75 million for most agricultural industries

Note that about one-fourth of industries have a size standard that is different from these levels. They vary from $0.75 million to $28.5 million for size standards based on average annual revenues and from 100 to 1500 employees for size standards based on number of employees.

With few exceptions, all federal agencies, and many state and local governments, use the size standards established by SBA. You can search for further information and for loan opportunities on the Small Business Administration's website.

Individuals

An individual submits a grant on their behalf, and not on behalf of a company, organization, institution, or government. Individuals sign the grant application and its associated certifications and assurances that are necessary to fulfill the requirements of the application process. So, if you register as an Individual, you will only be able to apply to grant opportunities that are open to individuals. An individual cannot submit a grant application to a grant opportunity that is just open to organizations.

Grants.gov now offers you even more help with finding and applying for federal grants. The self-help web portal (iPortal): www.grants.gov/iportal is yet another entry point to live 24 hour assistance for Grants.gov. Visit the Grants.gov homepage or Contact Us page to access the self-help iportal.

Foundations

- Sprint Foundation – Sprint Ahead for Education is a national grant program for character education. It awards grants to school districts ($25,000) and individual schools ($5,000) to fund the purchase of resource materials, supplies, equipment, and software that facilitates and encourages character education among K-12 students. With a national reach, the program is open to all US public schools (K-12) and US public school districts.

- Starbucks Foundation – This program helps young social entrepreneurs improve communities around the world through new ideas, volunteerism and civic action. Grants up to $1,000 are available to programs that help youth develop these skills.

CRITERIA FOR A GOOD GRANT PROPOSAL

Most funding agencies apply similar criteria to the evaluation of proposals. We discuss these below. It is important to address these criteria directly in your case for support. A proposal which fails to meet them will be rejected regardless of the quality of its source. Otherwise, there is a danger of discriminating unfairly in favour of well-known applicants.

Major criteria

Here are the major criteria against which your proposal will be judged. Read through your case for support repeatedly, and ask whether the answers to the questions below are clear, even to a non-expert.

- *Does the proposal address a well-formulated problem?*
- *Is it a research problem,* or is it just a routine application of known techniques?
- *Is it an important problem, whose solution will have useful effects?*
- *Is special funding necessary to solve the problem, or to solve it quickly enough,* or could it be solved using the normal resources of a well-found laboratory?
- *Do the proposers have a good idea on which to base their work?* The proposal must explain the idea in sufficient detail to convince the reader that the idea has some substance, and should explain why there is reason to believe that it is indeed a good idea. It is absolutely not enough merely to identify a wish-list of desirable goals (a very common fault). There must be significant technical substance to the proposal.
- *Does the proposal explain clearly what work will be done?* Does it explain what results are expected and how they will be evaluated? How would it be possible to judge whether the work was successful?
- *Is there evidence that the proposers know about the work that others have done on the problem?* This evidence may take the form of a short review as well as representative references.
- *Do the proposers have a good track record, both of doing good research and of publishing it?* A representative selection of relevant publications by the proposers should be cited. Absence of a track record is clearly not a disqualifying characteristic, especially in the case of young researchers, but a consistent failure to publish raises question marks.

Secondary criteria

Some secondary criteria may be applied to separate closely-matched proposals. It is often essentially impossible to distinguish in a truly objective manner among such proposals and it is sad that it is necessary to do so. The criteria are ambiguous and conflict with each other, so the committee simply has to use its best judgement in making its recommendations.

- An applicant with little existing funding may deserve to be placed ahead of a well-funded one. On the other hand, existing funding provides evidence of a good track record.

- There is merit in funding a proposal to keep a strong research team together; but it is also important to give priority to new researchers in the field.

- An attempt is made to maintain a reasonable balance between different research areas, where this is possible.

- Evidence of industrial interest in a proposal, and of its potential for future exploitation will usually count in its favour. The closer the research is to producing a product the more industrial involvement is required and this should usually include some industrial contribution to the project. The case for support should include some 'route to market' plan, i.e. you should have thought about how the research will eventually become a product --- identifying an industrial partner is usually part of such a plan.

- A proposal will benefit if it is seen to address recommendations of Technology Foresight. It is worth looking at the relevant Foresight Panel reports and including quotes in your case for support that relate to your proposal.

Cost-effectiveness

Finally, the programme manager tries to ensure that his or her budget is to be used in a cost-effective manner. Each proposal which has some chance of being funded is examined, and the programme manager may lop costs off an apparently over-expensive project.Such cost reduction is likely to happen if the major costs of staff and equipment are not given clear, individual justification.

COMMON SHORTCOMINGS

Here are some of the ways in which proposals often fail to meet these criteria.

- *It is not clear what question is being addressed by the proposal.* In particular, it is not clear what the outcome of the research might be, or what would constitute success or failure. It is vital to discuss what contribution to human knowledge would be made by the research.

- *The question being addressed is woolly or ill-formed.* The committee are looking for evidence of clear thinking both in the formulation of the problem and in the planned attack on it.

- *It is not clear why the question is worth addressing.* The proposal must be well motivated.

- *The proposal is just a routine application of known techniques.* Research funding agencies are interested in funding research rather than development. Industry are expected to fund development work. The LINK scheme is appropriate for proposals which combine both research and development. If the development would benefit another research field, rather than industry, then look to the funding agencies of that field.

- *Industry ought to be doing it instead.* If the work is 'near market' then it should be done by industry or industry or venture capital should be funding you to do it. If no industry is interested then the prima facie assumption is that the product has no commercial value.

- *There is no evidence that the proposers will succeed where others have failed.* It is easy enough to write a proposal with an exciting-sounding wish-list of hoped-for achievements, but you must substantiate your goals with solid evidence of why you have a good chance of achieving them.

This evidence generally takes two main forms:

   o "We have an idea". In this case, you should sketch the idea, and describe preliminary work you have done which shows that it is indeed a good idea. You are unlikely to get funding without such evidence. It is not good saying, "give us the money and we will start thinking about this problem".

   o "We have a good track record". Include a selective list of publications, and perhaps include a short paper (preferably a published one) which gives more background, as an appendix. If you make it clear that it is an appendix, you won't usually fall foul of any length limits.

- *A new idea is claimed but insufficient technical details of the idea are given for the committee to be able to judge whether it looks promising.* Since the committee cannot be expert in all areas there is a danger of overwhelming them with technical details, but it is better to err by overwhelming them than by underwhelming them. They will usually get an expert referee to evaluate your idea.

- *The proposers seem unaware of related research.* Related work must be mentioned, if only to be dismissed. Otherwise, the committee will think that the proposers are ignorant and, therefore, not the best group to fund. The case for support should have a list of references like any paper, and you should look at it to check it has a balanced feel - your referee will do so. Do not make the mistake of giving references only to your own work!

- *The proposed research has already been done - or appears to have been done*. Rival solutions must be discussed and their inadequacies revealed.

- *The proposal is badly presented, or incomprehensible to all but an expert in the field*. Remember that your proposal will be read by non-experts as well as (hopefully) experts. A good proposal is simultaneously comprehensible to non-experts, while also convincing experts that you know your subject. Keep highly-technical material in well-signposted section(s); avoid it in the introduction.

- *The proposers seem to be attempting too much for the funding requested and time-scale envisaged*. Such lack of realism may reflect a poor understanding of the problem or poor research methodology.

- *The proposal is too expensive for the probable gain*. If it is easy to see how to cut the request for people/equipment/travel, etc. to something more reasonable then it might be awarded in reduced form. More likely, it will be rejected.

- *The proposers institution should be funding it*. Research agencies will usually only fund research that requires resources beyond that which might be expected in a "well-found laboratory" --- indeed, this is part of the charter of the research councils. If it looks like your proposal might be done by a PhD student on the departmental computer then that is what should happen. If the proposer's laboratory is not "well-found" then this is taken to be a vote of no-confidence in the proposer by his/her institution.

Doubtless there are other common grounds for failure that have been omitted. If you know of any please let us know.

Often, one can tell from independent knowledge of the proposers or by reading between the lines of the proposal, that the criteria could have been met if a little bit more thought had gone into the proposal. There is a clear question being addressed by the research, but the proposers failed to clarify what it was. The proposers are aware of related research, but they failed to discuss it in the proposal. The proposers do have some clear technical ideas, but they thought it inappropriate to go into such detail in the proposal. Unfortunately, there is a limit to which a funding agencies can give such cases the benefit of the doubt. It is not fair for referees to overlook shortcomings in proposals of which they have personal knowledge if similar shortcomings are not overlooked in proposals which they have not encountered before. In any case, proposals which *do* meet the criteria deserve precedence.

CONCLUSION

We hope that this document will help you to write better grant proposals, and hence to be more successful in obtaining funds for your research. The basic set-up of peer-reviewed grants of limited duration is a sensible one. It compels researchers regularly to review and re-justify the direction of their work. Behind poorly presented grant proposals often lie poorly-reasoned research plans.

Government grants for women. http://www.womensnet.net/ApplyForAmberGrants.aspx

FOUNDATION GRANT DIRECTORY

Delaware Center for the Contemporary Arts, Inc.

200 South Madison Street

Wilmington , DE 19801

302-656-6466

http://www.thedcca.org

Please contact the foundation for more information about their grants and guidelines.

_____

Delaware Community Foundation

Suite 115 , 100 W. 10Th Street

Wilmington , DE 19801

302-571-8004

http://www.delcf.org/

Please contact the foundation for more information about their grants and guidelines.

_____

International Reading Association, Inc.

800 Barksdale Road, P.O. Box 8139

Newark , DE 19714

302-731-1600

http://www.reading.org

Please contact the foundation for more information about their grants and guidelines.

Raskob Foundation for Catholic Activities, Inc.

10 Montchanin Road, P.O. Box 4019

Wilimington , DE 19807

302-655-4440

http://www.rfca.org

Please contact the foundation for more information about their grants and guidelines.

Rodel Foundation of Delaware

100 West 10th Street, Suite 704

Wilmington , DE 19801

302-504-5254

http://www.rodelfoundationde.org

Please contact the foundation for more information about their grants and guidelines.

Social Venture Partners Delware, Inc.

100 West 10th Street, Suite 609

Wilmington , DE 19801

302-778-2691

http://www.svpde.org

Please contact the foundation for more information about their grants and guidelines.

The American Gift Fund

4550 New Linden Hill Road , Suite 200

Wilmington , DE 19808

800-240-4248

http://www.giftfund.org

Please contact the foundation for more information about their grants and guidelines.

The Brandywiners Ltd.

P.O. Box 248

Mountchanin , DE 19710

302-478-3355

http://www.brandywiners.org

Please contact the foundation for more information about their grants and guidelines.

FOUNDATION GRANT DIRECTORY

The MBNA Foundation

1100 North King Street

Wilmington, DE 19884

800-410-6262

http://www.mbnafoundation.org

Please contact the foundation for more information about their grants and guidelines.

The WSFS Bank Foundation

500 Delaware Avenue

Wilmington, DE 19801

302-792-6000

http://www.wsfsbank.com/

Please contact the foundation for more information about their grants and guidelines.

SCHOLARSHIPS/GRANTS FOR EDUCATION

1. *2012 Grants for Moms - You May Qualify for a Grant*

www.*collegegrants*.classesusa.com/

2. *Grants For Single Mothers*

mothers-grants.*educationgrant*.com
Single Mothers May Qualify For **Grants** Scholarships & Financial Aid

3. *Grants For Single Mothers Info | EducationConnection.com*

www.*educationconnection.com*/
Grants, Scholarships, Student Loans May Be Available if You Qualify.

4. Grants for Single Mothers *- Single Mother Guide*

singlemother*guide.com/**grants-for-single-mothers**
College Scholarships And Grants For Single Mothers *- Scholarships...*
www.*scholarships.com*..College Scholarships and *Grants for Single Mothers*. Single mothers must spend time with children, run errands and work long hours to provide for their families.

5. Grants For Single Mothers *Single Mom Resources*

www.**grantsforsinglemothers**.net
Grants For Single Mothers is a dedicated site to assist single moms with financial, career, family and educational matters.

6. Grants for Single Mothers *and Fathers - Single Parents*

singleparents.about.com
Grants for single mothers and fathers are usually awarded based on financial need, and do not have to be paid back. Find out which grants are available to*...*

7. Grants for Single Mothers *EducationGrant.com*

www.educationgrant.com/grants/grants-for-single-mothers

8. Grant For Single Mothers

9. Grants For Single Mothers *- **Christian Mommies***

*www.christian-mommies.com/...for-**moms**/**grants-for-single-mothers***

If you are a single mom and struggling to get by, you are not alone. Whether you are going through a divorce or the father is absent most *single mother* face the obstacles and need help.

10. Grants for Single Mothers *- **School Grants***

*www.school**grants**blog.com/**grants-for-single-mothers***

Grants for single mothers include housing grants, educational grants, transport grants and many other financial assistance.

CHAPTER 7

Business Entity Types

C Corporations

- Independent legal and tax structures separate from their owners.
- Help separate your personal assets from your business debts.
- No limit to the number of shareholders.
- Taxed on corporate profits and shareholder dividends.
- Must hold annual meetings and record meeting minutes.

Limited Liability Companies (LLCs)

- Independent legal structures separate from their owners.
- Help separate your personal assets from your business debts.
- Taxed similarly to a sole proprietorship (if one owner) or a partnership (if multiple owners).
- No limit to the number of owners.
- Not required to hold annual meetings or record minutes.
- Governed by operating agreements.

Partnerships

- Partners remain personally liable for lawsuits filed against the business.
- Usually no state filing required to form a partnership.
- Easy to form and operate.
- Owners report their share of profit and loss in the company on their personal tax returns.

S Corporations

- Independent legal and tax structures separate from their owners.

- Help separate your personal assets from your business debts.
- Owners report their share of profit and loss in the company on their personal tax returns.
- Limits on number of shareholders, who must be U.S. citizens or residents.
- Must hold annual meetings and record meeting minutes.

Sole Proprietorships

- Owner remains personally liable for lawsuits filed against the business.
- No state filing required to form a sole proprietorship.
- Easy to form and operate.
- Owner reports business profit and loss on their personal tax return.

Forming a limited liability company (LLC). **An LLC is a good way to "take off" your personal assets from your company's liabilities**, offering protection for your personal assets in the event of a judgment against your business. For this reason, it's a better fit for many owners than a sole proprietorship or a general partnership.

A limited liability company (LLC) also has certain tax advantages. The business itself is not responsible for taxes on its profits. Instead, the LLC's owners, known as "members," report their share of business profit and loss on their personal tax returns, similar to tax reporting for a general partnership. This is known as "pass-through" taxation.

The LLC Advantage

In short, the limited liability company business structure has many advantages, including:

- **Pass-through taxes.** There's no need to file a corporate tax return. Owners report their share of profit and loss on their individual tax returns.
- **No residency requirement.** Owners need not be U.S. citizens or permanent residents.
- **Legal protection.** Owners have limited liability for business debts and obligations.

- **Enhanced credibility.** Partners, suppliers and lenders may look more favorably on your business when you've formed an LLC.

Quick view: LLC vs. Corporation

Advantages of an LLC	Advantages of a Corporation
• no limit on the number of owners • profit and loss are passed through to the owners' individual tax returns • no annual meeting or minute book requirements	• may issue shares of stock to attract investors • corporate income splitting may help lower overall tax liability
Disadvantages of an LLC	**Disadvantages of a Corporation**
• cannot engage in corporate income splitting to lower tax liability • cannot issue stock	• double taxation of corporate profits and shareholder dividends • must hold annual meetings and record minutes • S Corporations have restrictions on number of owners

The Professional Corporation (PC) and Professional Limited Liability Company (PLLC) are the formations of choice for many business owners who work in accounting, law, medicine, architecture, engineering and related fields. These business entities can help licensed professionals protect their personal assets against lawsuits brought against their practices.

State laws vary, but PCs and PLLCs usually share these characteristics:

- Owners are generally required to be licensed in the same profession.
- Proof of licensing is often required for state approval.

- Industry-specific regulations may apply to your company name.
- States may require entity-specific endings for your company name ("PC" for a Professional Corporation and "PLLC" for a Professional Limited Liability Company, for example).

It's important to note that by forming a Professional Corporation or Professional Limited Liability Company, owners are not free from personal liability for malpractice or other suits brought against them. However, these formation types do protect owners from the malpractice of other owners within the company. Be aware, too, that not all states recognize the PLLC entity.

In addition, PCs and PLLCs are taxed differently. PCs are generally taxed like a C-Corporation, with the PC paying taxes at the corporate rate, which can lead to double taxation. PLLCs, on the other hand, are taxed like LLCs, which generally have pass-through taxation of the members. You may wish to consult with a tax advisor before forming either a PC or PLLC to determine the best tax treatment for your company.

Forming these companies may also require additional steps on the part of the owners. Along with approval from the Secretary of State, professional entities often must seek approval of their formation documents from the state professional licensing body.

Nonprofit corporations enjoy the following advantages:

- **Limited liability protection.** Directors and officers are not personally liable for the organization's debts and liabilities.
- **Perpetual existence.** The corporation continues even if a director leaves the business or passes away.
- **Eligibility for grants.** Nonprofits may be eligible for certain public and private grants.

While nonprofits are bound by different state laws than for-profit enterprises, in general their formation processes are quite similar. Like a regular corporation, nonprofits must file Articles of Incorporation with the state in which they wish to incorporate.

In addition, the IRS requires organizations seeking tax-exempt status to file Form 1023. Several states also require organizations to file for state-level tax-exemption. The nonprofit status most commonly sought by organizations is the Internal Revenue Service's 501(c)(3) tax-exempt status. Organizations that qualify for 501(c)(3) status enjoy the following advantages:

- **Tax-exempt status.** Qualifying nonprofits can apply for federal and state tax-exempt status
- **Enhanced credibility.** Potential donors may be more inclined to give to an organization that has an official nonprofit status
- **Tax-deductible donations.** Donations made by individuals to the nonprofit corporation may be tax-deductible
- **Possible exemption.** from certain property taxes.
- **Reduced postage rates.**

By forming a **C Corporation**, business owners create a separate legal structure that helps shield their personal assets from judgments against the company. C Corporations have a specific structure that includes shareholders, directors, and officers.

The **C Corporation** is a time-tested business formation. It has many advantages, including:

- **Limited liability** for directors, officers, shareholders, and employees
- **Perpetual existence**, even if the owner leaves the company
- **Enhanced credibility** among suppliers and lenders
- **Unlimited growth potential** through the sale of stock
- **No limit** on the number of shareholders, although once the company has $10 million in assets and 500 shareholders, it is required to register with the SEC under the Securities Exchange Act of 1934
- **Certain tax advantages**, including tax-deductible business expenses

The C Corporation structure does have its drawbacks. For instance, a C Corporation's profits are taxed when earned and taxed again when distributed as shareholders' dividends, what's known as "double taxation." Shareholders in a C Corporation also can't deduct any corporate losses. To avoid these concerns, many small business owners choose to form an **S Corporation** instead.

What is a S Corporation?

This federal tax status enables companies to "pass through" their taxable income or losses to owners/investors in the business, according to their ownership stake in the business.

By default, companies that do not specify a tax status with the IRS are considered to be C Corporations - which means that they will be taxed as a C Corporation. On the other hand, **by electing S Corporation status, a corporation can eliminate the disadvantage of "double taxation" of corporate income and shareholder dividends** associated with the C Corporation tax status.

Say a corporation makes $300,000 in a given year - if it is an S Corporation, the business itself will not be taxed for that amount; instead, the company's shareholders will be required to pay taxes according to their share of the company. In this scenario, if the company has three shareholders, each with an equal share of company stock, each shareholder will pay taxes on $100,000.

If the C Corporation makes $300,000 in a year, then the company would pay taxes at the current federal corporate tax rate of about 34%. If the remaining profits of $198,000 are distributed to the three shareholders as dividends, each shareholder will pay taxes on $66,000 in dividend income at the current federal dividend tax rate of 15%.

S Corporations, like other types of corporate entities, also keep owners' personal assets safe from company debt and judgments against the business.

In short, the S Corporation status offers the following advantages:

- **Limited liability:** Company directors, officers, shareholders, and employees enjoy limited liability protection
- **Pass-through taxation:** Owners report their share of profit and loss on their individual tax returns
- **Elimination of double taxation of income:** Income is not taxed twice; once as corporate income and again as dividend income
- **Investment opportunities:** The company can attract investors through the sale of shares of stock
- **Perpetual existence:** The business continues to exist even if the owner leaves or dies
- **Once-a-year tax filing requirement** (vs. quarterly for a C Corporation)

Most state, county, and local governments require companies to have the right licenses and permits in place before they open their doors. There are more than 150,000 filing jurisdictions across the country, all with their own requirements. Depending on your particular industry and where you operate, any number of licenses and permits may apply to your business.

Examples of commonly required licenses and permits include:

- General business licenses
- Tax registrations
- Health permits
- State-issued occupational licenses
- Liquor licenses
- Lottery licenses
- Reseller's licenses
- Zoning and land-use permits
- Health department permits

Failure to obtain and renew the correct business licenses and permits can result in fines, notices, and forced closure of your business. Understandably, many business owners find identifying and applying for the right business licenses and permits to be a time-consuming, complicated, and even an overwhelming process.

Pay Your Delaware Taxes the Easy Way

Delaware corporations and Limited Liability Companies (LLCs) must pay annual franchise taxes to the state. Delaware corporations must also file an annual report.

Certificate of Good Standing, also called a "Certificate of Existence" or "Certificate of Authorization," is a state-issued document that shows that your corporation or limited liability company (LLC) has met its statutory requirements and is authorized to do business in that state. Think of it as a kind of 'snapshot' of your business's compliance status.

Among other things, a Certificate of Good Standing confirms that your business:

- Is up-to-date on its state fee payments
- Has filed an annual report
- Has paid its franchise taxes

There's a good chance you'll need to secure a Certificate of Good Standing from time to time during the life of your business. Many companies request a Certificate of Good Standing occasionally for their own records. A Certificate of Good Standing may also be required by:

- State governments, if you're applying for foreign qualification there
- Lenders, when you're trying to obtain financing
- Banks, for certain transactions
- Potential business partners or investors

You may need to present your Certificate of Good Standing in order to renew specific licenses or permits, and a Certificate of Good Standing is also important evidence when it comes time to sell your business. In addition, if you are looking to register to do business in additional states, those states may ask for a copy of your Certificate of Good Standing.

Bylaws

State law requires all corporations to create a document outlining their organization and day-to-day operations. Called your corporate bylaws, it's one of your company's most important legal documents.

Among a number of other details, corporate bylaws generally contain:

- the structure of the organization
- the duties and responsibilities of a corporation's members
- details about the board of directors
- information about when and where directors' and shareholders' meetings will be held
- a list of committees

Much the same, limited liability companies (LLCs) in many states are required to have something called an operating agreement; a document that provides a framework for their operation.

Operating agreements typically contain information about:

- members' percentages of ownership
- members' rights and responsibilities
- members' voting powers
- allocation of profits and losses
- management details
- the fiduciary duties of members and managers

Corporations and LLCs aren't required to file their bylaws or operating agreements with the Secretary of State. Still, you should have them in place as soon as you've incorporated or formed your LLC, because these documents are often requested by:

- lenders, when you're trying to obtain financing
- banks, when you're opening a business checking account
- potential business partners or investors
- attorneys and accountants

What do company records, include:

- Articles of Incorporation
- Bylaws
- Meeting minutes
- Stock certificates
- Stock transfer ledgers
- Corporate resolutions
- Written consents
- Federal/state documents

- Business licenses

Keeping Your Business Records Up-to-Date

Whenever your corporation or limited liability company undertakes certain important actions those actions must be memorialized in resolutions of the board of directors, shareholders or LLC members.

In general, these actions can be approved in one of two ways: by having owners, directors, or members vote on a resolution at a meeting, or, if the company does not hold a meeting, through a document known as a "written consent." To enact a change, a written consent is drafted and the company representatives who would have approved the resolution at a meeting sign the document in turn.

Written consents are important evidence for many business purposes, including opening company bank accounts.

They are typically needed when:

- Changing LLC members or managers
- Changing corporate officers or directors
- Issuing stock to a new shareholder
- Opening a company bank account
- Merging the company with another company
- Selling the business or a substantial portion of its assets

Who needs Compliance Coaching?

- You are starting a corporation or LLC for the first time.
- You are too busy to worry about tracking due dates.
- You want to keep up to date and accurate documentation on file for your business.
- You would like a go-to person who you can turn to for help when you need it.
- You want personalized service from an expert who understands what you need.

- You missed a due date in the past and had to deal with late fees, fines, and penalties.
- You are confused about the steps to take after incorporating a business.

Stock Certificates

Stock certificates are official documents issued by a company to its shareholders that provide evidence of how much of an ownership stake they have in the corporation. Limited liability companies (LLCs)have a similar document, called a membership certificate, which they issue to their members.

In general, both documents include the following information:

- Name of the corporation or LLC
- State where it was formed
- Number of units issued
- Recipient's name

Stock & membership certificates serve as an important record for corporate ledgers and registers. They also help increase company reputability by providing owners with a piece of official documentation representing their ownership stake in the business.

How to apply for an EIN number?

An EIN federal nine-digit number identifies a business entity. The Internal Revenue Service (IRS) issues EINs and requires their use on all tax filings during the entire life of a business.

The IRS generally requires the following types of businesses to obtain an EIN:

- All corporations
- All Limited Liability Companies (LLCs) with more than one member
- Any business that hires employees, including sole proprietorships and single-member LLCs

- - 95 - -

Many nonprofit organizations, as well as trusts and certain co-ops, must also have an EIN. If a business has changed its formation type or emerged from bankruptcy, it is typically required to apply for a new Employer Identification Number (EIN).

For many business owners, obtaining an EIN is one of the first things they do after incorporating or forming an LLC. Along with tax filings, businesses often need an EIN in order to:

- open business checking accounts
- establish accounts with certain vendors

Sometimes you'll see the Employer Identification Number referred to as a Tax Identification Number (TIN) or Federal Employer Identification Number (FEIN). As a general rule, it's good for all businesses, with the exception of sole proprietorships without employees, to have an EIN.

Businesses close for many reasons, but it's not enough for corporations or LLCs to simply shut their doors. If you have gone out of business, you need to officially dissolve your corporation or LLC with the state.

How to Close Your Business

Until the Secretary of State's office is aware that your company is no longer in operation, you are still liable for annual report filings, franchise tax payments and other obligations.

It's critical that you formally dissolve your company, because letting it lapse or allowing the state to dissolve it involuntarily could create a number of problems, including:

- Personal liability for judgments against the business
- Expensive state-assessed penalties and fees
- Unnecessary registered agent service payments

The best way to put a stop to these obligations is to file Articles of Dissolution with the state. By doing so, you will end your company's existence in your state of incorporation and as well as any other states where you are qualified to do business. Formal dissolution also gives you the chance to tie up other loose ends, such as ending your obligation to maintain a registered agent service.

Registered Agent

Corporations and Limited Liability Companies (LLCs) are required by state law to have an address where they can receive important legal and tax documents during all business hours. The person or firm receiving these documents is known as the company's "Registered Agent." For reasons including convenience and reliability, most established businesses choose a third-party Registered Agent (like The Company Corporation) to handle their legal documents.

Corporate Name Check

The success of your business depends to some degree on your ability to set yourself apart from the competition. A good first step is choosing the right business name.

Even if you're not ready to form a corporation or LLC, The Company Corporation can reserve your business name in the state where you intend to form your company. Simply tell us what name you want to reserve and we'll conduct a search of the state records to make sure it's available. If it is, we will reserve your name of choice and hold it for you as long as state rules allow, preventing other companies from registering their businesses under the same name.

Be sure to choose your company name carefully. The name should be descriptive of your business activities, and it must be unique - it can't be confused with that of any other corporation, limited liability company (LLC) or partnership in your intended state of formation.

Keep in mind that:

- State laws vary widely when it comes to business name reservations. Our Business Specialists can give you more details about the process and how to successfully reserve your name.
- Reserving a name does not create a legal business structure. For that, you'll need to incorporate or form an LLC.
- Even if the state approves your name reservation, there's no guarantee that it will accept the name when you decide to incorporate under that name.

In conclusion, preparing and filing annual reports for your company demands time, diligence and expense. Deadlines and filing requirements vary from state to state, and with annual reminders becoming a less-common courtesy, it's easy to be left in the dark about when your annual reports are due. Save time and reduce your chances of filing mishaps by outsourcing your annual report needs to your local accountant.

- Conduct an initial audit to ensure you are in good standing
- Track filing deadlines for your annual reports
- Prepare annual reports on your behalf and file the completed documents
- Update your company information

APPENDIX:

Starting Your Own Business: Quickly

"Writing Your Vision"

Most people will tell you that the greatest thing about working for themselves is that they don't have a boss. Technically they do, which is themselves, but not having another person to always tell them what to do is a great relief. Once you can make your own decisions and determine your daily behaviors on your, you can become much more efficient. It's no secret that several layers of management can make a company sluggish and lethargic, and not very productive. As your own boss, you can focus only on those things that directly impact your bottom line.

The second reason is that you get to make your own hours. Of course, this is a double- edged sword. One of the benefits of working in some jobs is that when the whistle blows, you're finished. Working your own hours means you sometimes work much longer than you normally would at a standard nine to give, but something about working for yourself makes them much more preferable.

The Pros

1. If your employer is letting you go, offering early retirement or using another euphemism for firing you, it may be hard to find another job immediately. Being in business for yourself allows you to immediately start working on making money, rather than proofreading your **resume.**

2. Without the middleman (a.k.a. your employer) you can charge significantly more for your services along the lines of what your employer was charging for your work.

3. You don't have to go whole hog into running your own business. You can try out your business on a part-time, evenings and weekends, basis while still working your current job.

4. It can be easier to pick up overtime if you no longer have to get your manager to sign off on it. If you run your own business, overtime is a matter of finding another client or customer.

5. The cost of working at home is much lower than for your employer: you don't have to pay to commute, you can eat inexpensively in your own kitchen and you only have to meet a dress code

when you'll actually be seeing a client. And, while this isn't particularly noble, you can avoid the constant birthday parties, baby showers and other office events that constantly drain your time and your wallet.

6. Just about all of the expenses associated with your business are tax deductible. Running your own business can make your tax burden significantly lower and a surprising number of things are considered business expenses, like conference registrations.

The Cons

1. While getting health insurance without an employer providing it isn't impossible, it can be pretty difficult — especially if you actually need. Pre-existing conditions can make it absolutely impossible to get health insurance on your own.

2. With a job, if you aren't quite on the ball one week, you still get paid. But if you fumble on your own business, you can wind up losing money. Even if you have a contract, sometimes things can go very wrong. An employer absorbs those problems, but can you do that if you're on your own?

3. There are some great jobs that simply aren't possible to do in a small business that you're just starting yourself. If you have one of those jobs and you like it, why mess with a good thing?

4. It's all well and good to jump off the deep end if no one's depending on your earnings. But if you have a family or other dependents, you have to be absolutely sure before you strike out on your own.

5. You have to buy your own equipment when you run your own business: no more company laptop — or printing out your personal stuff at work. A computer, a printer, maybe even a fax machine: you'll have to buy whatever you need for your home office.

6. There's no such thing as **vacation** time or sick leave when you run your own business. You can certainly take time off when you need to — after all, you're the boss — but you just don't get paid when you're not working.

7. While the flexibility of working for yourself can be nice, more and more employers are offering flex time and telecommuting options. You can have a lot of the benefits of working for yourself without having to give up a regular salary.

PERSONAL ASSESSMENT

Are You Ready to Start a Business? – A short personal assessment tool.

Being your own boss is wonderfully exciting, but isn't for everyone. Anyone considering starting a business needs first to consider if they are suited for it, personally and professionally.

There is no right or wrong answer to each of these questions. This is a self-evaluation to help you think through critical aspects of your personal and business readiness to be self-employed. It is designed to help you assess your reasons and qualifications for going into business, to help you set personal and business goals, consider if this is the right time to start a business, if you have the freedom, flexibility and resources to start a business, to consider your health and stamina, and how you will balance family and business.

SELF ASSESSMENT: Are You Ready To Be In Business?

1. Why do I want to start a business? OR Why am I in business?
2. Specifically, what kind of business do I want to start (or am I in)?
3. Why do I believe I can make this type of business work?
4. Why do I believe this type of business is sustainable?
5. What education, skill or experience do I have in this industry?
6. What is my true purpose and/or the **goal I hope to accomplish with this business**?
7. What is the **financial goal** I am seeking to achieve?
8. If I will need financing, do I have the resources and credit worthiness necessary to be eligible? [High credit score plus assets, collateral and good financial history.]
9. What are my strengths?
10. What are my weaknesses?
11. What is my physical, mental and emotional health and stamina?
12. What knowledge and skills do I have to start and control the day-to-day operations of a business?
13. Do I know and understand the technology necessary to be competitive in this business?

14. Do I have good judgment in people and ideas?

15. What sacrifices and **risks** am I willing to take to be successful?

16. What will it take for me to balance personal life and business demands?

ABOUT THE AUTHOR

(Author, Motivational and National Speaker of Black Speakers Bureau, Named as the Top 100 Businesses in the Mid-Atlantic Region, Life Coach, Job Coach, Business Consultant, Evangelist, and College Professor)

Alisha attended Delaware Technical and Community College (1995), where she earned an Associate's Degree in Early Childhood Education, later she attended Delaware State University (1987-1991), where she earned her Bachelor of Arts degree in Journalism/English. In 2000, she earned her Master's degree in Special Education. She is currently pursuing her PHD in Organizational Leadership and a second PHD in Biblical Studies, Christian Education and Counseling.

Alisha is a member of the National Association of Business Owners, The Delaware State Teacher's Education, The

Maryland State Teacher's Association, The National Teacher's Association, The Milton Chamber of Commerce, The Milton Historical Society, Friends of the Milton Library, 2nd Vice President for the NAACP, a trainer subcontractor for the State of DE, Member of the Office of Minority Women, Owner and CEO of Unlimited Expectations Training and Consulting, LLC, Civic Association of Cool Spring, a volunteer and mentor the Delaware Breast Coalition, Delaware State University Alumni, Delaware Technical and Community College Alumni, Wilmington College University Alumni, Participant Purses for Women Financial Literacy Program, Participant Score Program of DE, YWCA member, Editor for several books, Sunday School Teacher, Public School Educator, College Instructor, Sussex County Woman's Democratic Club, and 36th Democratic Party.

Alisha is a past instructor at Delaware Technical and Community College in Georgetown, DE and Delaware State University. She is a freelance writer for several Delaware Newspapers: Cape Gazette, Delaware State News, Coast Press, and the Sussex Post.

She has 15 years of experience as group facilitator and trainer focusing on coaching and learning. She has been a host to the Just You and the Floyd Potts blog talk radio show. In 2006, Ms. Broughton was hostesses for a commercial, Vote or Die, Sean "Puffy" Combs also known as P. Diddy, for BET television. Broughton conducts customized seminars for non-profits, businesses, churches, school districts and colleges. The trainings provide coaching and seminars for personal and professional growth. She specializes in the design and implementation of 1 of 2 trainings using team building tools. She has consulted and facilitated trainings for organizations within the United States. She has served on multiple committees at her church. Alisha loves God and places Him first in her life.

Broughton was recognized by the State of Maryland, the Pinder Group and Southwest Airlines, on Friday, May 4, 2012 at the University of Maryland College Park in Baltimore, Maryland, for her outstanding contributions to individuals in business. Each year the State of Maryland recognizes the Top 100 businesses within the Mid-Atlantic Region. Broughton has provided services to the State of Maryland and is to be commended for her accomplishments in the areas of: customized training, PR, grant writing, event planning, book editing and scholarship assistant. Broughton has volunteered 2,000 hours. Many of her hours have been unpaid. This is why she is being saluted as one of our outstanding business CEO's within our local region. Broughton stated, "I do realize if I give back to my community that my blessing is right around the corner. People see what I do and wonder, "Wow, she is loaded but they cannot even begin to see the sweat and hard work that goes beyond it. I thank my Heavenly Father for it. Without Him nothing would be possible. I believe as I decree things in the atmosphere they shall be so. I want to especially empower single mothers to come out of poverty, to dream big and aim high. Life has not always been easy, but I continue to move forward and Trust God. I live to make a difference. When I looked at my finances many said, "How can you start a business?" Even though the odds were against me, I knew God was for me."

Unlimited Expectations is a 8a Certified, Minority-Owned Business and a CCR Business for the State of Delaware. Business Description: Unlimited Expectations Training and Consulting, LLC. provides services to individuals, businesses, non-profits, schools and churches. Unlimited Expectations Training and Consulting, LLC. provides the following services: customized trainings to churches, schools and corporation, grant writing, proposals, assist in business plan writing, job coaching, resumes, wedding and event planning, spiritual coaching and life coaching, book editing, tutoring, scholarship assistance, author and motivational speaker. Unlimited Expectations creates and implements practices and systems that will improve your efficiency, revamp and refocus area and products which are currently stagnant; provide you with necessary details about unfamiliar markets and provide quick and educated solutions.

Broughton has recently started a faith-based non-profit agency called, Unlimited Expectations New Horizons, this non-profit agency focuses on job placement, life skills, computer classes, trainings, parenting classes, self-empowerment, prison entry inmates, after-school activities, youth activities and provides funding to individuals in the community to assist in paying their bills.

If you are interested in any of these services contact Alisha Broughton@ (302)-362-9369. Visit the Company's website at: www.unlimitedex.com.

2 0 1 2

SILVER

STEVIE® WINNER

STEVIE AWARDS FOR WOMEN IN BUSINESS

STEVIE AWARD

Press Release from the Stevie Awards
"STEVIE AWARDS FOR WOMEN IN BUSINESS"

Contact:
[Alisha Broughton]
[(302)-362-9369, alishabroughton@hotmail.com]

ALISHA BROUGHTON WINS AN EXTINGUISHED AWARD FOR WOMEN IN BUSINESS AS BEST MENTOR OF THE YEAR: MOTIVATIONAL SPEAKER, LIFE COACH AND BUSINESS COACH FOR STEVIE® AWARDS IN 2012 STEVIE AWARDS FOR WOMEN IN BUSINESS.

Winners Announced at Event in New York City

[Milton, DE] – November 10, 2012 – [Unlimited Expectations Training and Consulting Group] has been named the winner of a [Women in Business Award] Stevie® Award in the (**Best Mentor or the Year**): **Free Seminars by Alisha Broughton, Motivational Speaker/Life Coach,** category in the 9th annual Stevie Awards for Women in Business.

The Stevie Awards for Women in Business are the world's top honors for female entrepreneurs, executives, and the organizations they run. All individuals and organizations worldwide are eligible to submit nominations – public and private, for-profit and non-profit, large and small. The 2012 awards received entries from 17 nations and territories.

Nicknamed the Stevies for the Greek word for "crowned," the awards were presented to winners during a dinner at the Marriott Marquis Hotel in New York City. This year it will be held on Friday, November 9, 2012 in New York City.

More than 1,200 nominations from organizations of all sizes and in virtually every industry were submitted this year for consideration in a wide range of categories, including Entrepreneur of the Year, Executive of the Year, Company of the Year, Mentor of the Year, Women Helping Women, and Communications Campaign of the Year, among others. (Alisha Broughton) won in the **Best Mentor of the Year** category for Life and Job Coaching, and Mentoring.

[Unlimited Expectations Training and Consulting, LLC. proudly congratulates Alisha Broughton for all of her volunteer work in mentoring individuals in business, youth and organizations.]

Stevie Award winners were selected by more than 200 executives worldwide who participated in the judging process this year.

"I'm very pleased that we were able to conclude our tenth year of organizing Stevie Awards programs with a very successful Women in Business event," said Michael Gallagher, president and founder of the Stevie Awards. "This year's Stevie Award-winning women are the most accomplished, impressive group we've ever had. Their stories of success will be an inspiration to women around the globe who dream of starting and growing a business and making a difference in the world."

Details about the Stevie Awards for Women in Business and the list of Stevie Award winners are available at www.StevieAwards.com/Women.

About [Alisha Broughton]
[Alisha attended Delaware Technical and Community College (1995), where she earned an Associate's Degree in Early Childhood Education, later she attended Delaware State University (1987-1991), where she earned her Bachelor of Arts degree in Journalism/English. In 2000, she earned her Master's degree in Special Education from Wilmington University. She is currently pursuing her PHD in Organizational Leadership at Walden University and plans to earn her second PHD in Biblical Studies, Christian Education and Counseling through Friends International Bible College.]

About the Stevie Awards
Stevie Awards are conferred in four programs: The International Business Awards, The American Business Awards, the Stevie Awards for Women in Business, and the Stevie Awards for Sales & Customer Service. Honoring organizations of all types and sizes and the people behind them, the Stevies recognize outstanding performances in the workplace worldwide. Learn more about The Stevie Awards at www.StevieAwards.com.

###

CBID · R · grei**BO** media

TOP100 MBEs

THANK YOU for supporting the 6th Annual Top 100 MBE® Awards Ceremony.

2012 Top 100 MBE Winners

Hall of Fame Winners

100 businesses from the mid-Atlantic region were honored along with 10 Hall of Fame recipients and Legacy of Leadership Award winners Mayor Stephanie Rawlings-Blake, Comptroller Peter Franchot, Business Legends Dr. Marsha Firestone, Sung Kil Lee, Special Advocacy Award winner – Ken Clark; Prestige Award winner Charles "Choo" Smith; and Congressman Parren J. Mitchell Vanguard for Justice winners Arnold Jolivet and Roger Campos.

Special thanks to our Sponsors and Partners. Congratulations to the winners of the State Farm gift cards and Lunch with the Executive; Southwest Airline tickets, and to Sharon Gilbert – the winner of our Ultimate Marketing Makeover. *For a complete list of winners, sponsors and partners, please visit www.top100mbe.com.*

Special Award Winners

Photos will be posted next week and look for the Hall of Fame Tour information in the coming weeks.

Pardon Us.....

We appreciate your patience through the mystery of the missing name badges and through the parking situation. Please accept our apology for the inconvenience.

If you paid the Marriott for parking, please provide us with a receipt or request for reimbursement. Mail request with your contact information to: Top 100 MBE Awards, 6030 Daybreak Circle, Suite 150-155, Clarksville, Maryland 21029. Please place the words Parking Reimbursement on your envelope.

Processional of Dignitaries

Coach Alisha Broughton's Seminar Pictures

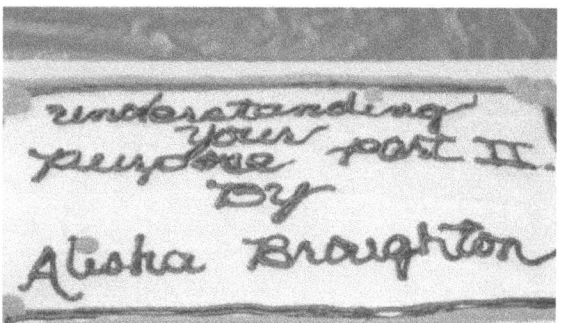

www.ingramcontent.com/pod-product-compliance
Lightning Source LLC
Chambersburg PA
CBHW081548220326
41598CB00036B/6604